mar·ket·ing

*Everything you need to know
in a bite-sized pocket guide.*

Written by:

Sonya Gonzalez Mier

First Printing Edition, 2023
978-1-7395037-1-0

Advisor: Ray Hilditch
Illustration by Jonah Price
Proofreading by Yuseok Han
Proofreading by Gregory Newton Brown

To Ray, who introduced me to the wonderful world of marketing.

To my mum, who allowed me not to become an accountant.

To Michael, who made me the Marketer I am today.

Table of Contents

Foreword

To the point. Powerful. Actionable.

In a world where marketing is sometimes a blurry and often misunderstood concept, this book is refreshing. Its succinct chapters provide a fantastic overview of marketing, one that will help you increase your marketing literacy fast and be there for you throughout your career as an invaluable resource.

I had the privilege to work in marketing throughout a career that included roles at P&G, L'Oréal, Nestlé, and that covered the full spectrum of the marketing mix. I also had the pleasure of being appointed a fellow of both the Marketing Society and the Marketing Academy, organisations dedicated to inspiring and developing the marketing leaders of tomorrow, and I currently serve as a marketing and strategy teaching fellow at Aston University.

I've always believed that marketing should be a core function in any business, as it's dedicated to the consumer. Marketers are the consumer's voice inside the organisation, serving them externally with products they love and can rely on. Consistency is key to achieving this. That's why I've always considered marketing as a science—a social science that follows processes and has rules to drive efficiency and predictable outcomes.

Not understanding this basic principle can make marketing frustrating. A lack of structure and science-backed approaches often leads to ego-fuelled debates that might serve the people in the room but no one else.

Fundamentally, marketing should be exciting! It's stimulating and, when done right, very rewarding. Understanding consumers to make a difference in their life is like a puzzle that keeps changing. It's a game that always gives you new challenges. And when done properly, it positively impacts the business, consumers, and yourself.

This book practices what it preaches: it puts you, the consumer, at its heart and gives you the foundational tools to build sound marketing strategies that drive results. What makes this approach even more powerful is that it comes from Sonya. I have had the pleasure to work with Sonya and to witness her outstanding career. Her rich array of consumer experiences in fast-moving consumer goods and technology, both on the client and agency side, and both at big and small brands, coupled with her relentless passion for sharing her knowledge, makes this book stand out.

A profound desire to coach, to give tips, and to provide shortcuts to enable you to be successful is the spirit emanating from these pages. With Sonya's generous support, I have no doubt that you will find the tools and information you need to approach the science of marketing as clearly and effectively as you can. Becoming the marketer you've always wanted to be can start right here.

Enjoy the read. Enjoy the ride.
Michael Inpong

Fellow of the Marketing Society
Fellow of the Marketing Academy
Marketing and Strategy Teaching Fellow at Aston University

Preface

When I uploaded my first video, talking about how I developed and marketed sticky tape, I didn't think anyone would care. But millions of views proved me wrong. Not only did people think it was fascinating, but they also took the chance to voice their frustrations.

Little did I know then that marketing was a sore point for many.

As someone who's worked in the field for almost a decade, I'm keenly aware of how much of a walled garden it can be. The amount of jargon alone drives even long-standing marketers into despair, let alone outsiders like my mum, who, to this day, can't describe what I do. Yet, marketing is everywhere around us. Anyone who's worked in a business, bought from, or started one has come in touch with it.

Some of the most common questions I often hear in conversations are: 'Where do I even start' or 'Should I just start posting'? And while I've done my best to provide a guiding light, it is true that until now, the choices for learning the basics were limited to heavy academic literature or entrepreneurial 'how to do business' books.

So, I wrote the book that I wish had already existed when I started my marketing career.

This book aims to consolidate the most important marketing concepts for business owners, students, and anyone interested in the field. Through engaging and accessible chapters, we will explore each central concept, arriving at a bite-sized pocket guide to marketing. It incudes practical tools deployed by companies like

Unilever, P&G, Henkel, Nestle, L'Oréal, TikTok, and academic literature, offering actionable ideas and frameworks that can be easily applied, no matter what marketing field readers are interested in.

The book is divided into 8 sections, following the marketing path to develop a comprehensive strategy. In addition, each chapter can act as a stand-alone reference point on topics the reader might need a refresher on.

Before getting into the details of 'what' and 'how', the **Fundamental** chapters aim to answer common questions and set the overall context. We discuss how marketing has evolved over the last century, what we define as marketing, the importance of ethics, and how to set a marketing budget.

Every good marketing strategy starts with a strong **Analysis**. However, this step can often be overwhelming in a world increasingly cluttered with data. A few handy frameworks and tips on how to conduct effective market research can provide a guiding light to the data jungle and help avoid pitfalls along the way.

Now that we know the market and consumer, we get to the creative part of marketing - **Brand Building**. When asked in the past if marketing is an art or a science, my favourite answer is to sit on the fence and answer: 'Both'! Marketing is very data-driven; however, what we do with these insights and how we translate them into products and services can be seen as an art. In this section, we talk about the key differences between branding and marketing; how to differentiate insights from mere data points; and how, based on this, to choose the right positioning in the market.

Next up is the **Marketing Mix**. Whether you've heard of the 4, 5, 6, or 7 Ps, they are one of the more well-known concepts in the field. We explore their importance in developing a coherent strategy and dive into each to understand how they can be applied to small, medium, and large businesses based on real-life examples.

An often overlooked but critical part of marketing is how the field of behavioural psychology plays a vital part in explaining certain **Consumer Behaviours**. Marketing works so well on us because most of it is deeply rooted in the traits ingrained in us through our societal and cultural environment. Understanding a few essential concepts can make all the difference in gaining a better understanding of our consumers and therefore guide us in designing better marketing strategies in the long term.

Communication is the most visible and well-known part of marketing. Here we will review how to choose from the various advertising channels based on the marketing objectives and then dive into the most common channels one by one, exploring their benefits, limitations, and best practice tips on designing effective marketing campaigns that drive results.

As an old boss of mine used to say: 'What use is the prettiest marketing strategy if our consumers can't buy the product'? **Distribution** might be one of the last steps of any marketing strategy, but it is undoubtedly one of the most important. With the rise of eCommerce and online platforms, barriers of entry to a market are slowly getting democratised, allowing small and medium businesses to become more available than ever. This section will explore the most common distribution channels and provide a guide on designing an effective distribution strategy.

Last, but certainly not least, we touch on **Measurement**. No strategy is complete without an ongoing analysis of key performance indicators that allow marketers and businesses to adjust. Consumers vote with their purses, and keeping an eye on the market to stay on top of rapidly changing business environments is mandatory. We will review the importance of choosing the right KPIs and how to build effective measurement processes that provide the right insights at the right time.

This has been a passion project of mine, and I sincerely hope it will become a handy pocket guide to help you navigate the world of marketing.

Sincerely,
Sonya Gonzalez Mier

I
Marketing Fundamentals

Chapter 1

The History of Marketing

Marketing has come a long way since its inception in the early 1900s. The field has evolved tremendously regarding techniques, strategies, and the public perception of marketing. Before we continue to learn the most important tools and strategies, we will review the history of marketing and how it has evolved over the past 100 years.

Marketing in the Early 1900s

Marketing as we know it today only came into existence in the early 1900s. Advertising was in its infancy and was limited mainly to print media such as newspapers and magazines. The focus of advertising was primarily on product features and benefits, with little consideration given to the needs and desires of the consumer.

One of the pioneers of modern marketing was John Wanamaker, a Philadelphia department store owner credited with coining the phrase: 'Half the money I spend on advertising is wasted; the trouble is, I don't know which half'. Wanamaker was one of the first retailers to advertise his products and services. He was known for his innovative marketing tactics, such as offering money-back guarantees on products.

Marketing in the Mid-1900s

By the mid-1900s, marketing had evolved considerably. The rise of radio and television brought new opportunities for advertisers to reach a wider audience. Advertisers began to focus on creating emotional connections with consumers rather than just promoting product features and benefits.

One of the most famous advertising campaigns was the 'Think Small' campaign for Volkswagen, created by the ad agency Doyle Dane Bernbach. The campaign focused on the small size of the Volkswagen Beetle and used humour and wit to make the car seem appealing to consumers.

Marketing Now

Since the mid-1900s, marketing has continued to evolve. The rise of the internet and social media brought new opportunities for marketers to reach consumers innovatively. Brands began to focus on creating consumer experiences rather than just selling products.

One example is the Nike+ Running app, which allows users to track and share their runs with friends on social media. The app creates a sense of community around the Nike brand and encourages users to engage with the brand on a deeper level.

Perception of Marketing in Public

As marketing evolved, its public perception did as well. In the early days, advertising was primarily seen as a necessary evil. Consumers were sceptical of ads and were not easily swayed by them.

In the mid-1900s, the rise of emotional advertising helped change the public perception of marketing. Ads became more creative and entertaining, and consumers began viewing them as entertainment rather than an annoyance.

Today, the public perception of marketing is more mixed. While consumers are still drawn to creative and entertaining ads, they are also more aware of some advertisers' manipulative tactics. There is a growing demand for transparency and authenticity in marketing, and consumers quickly call out brands that engage in unethical practices.

The Biggest Trends Today

Marketers have a lot to learn from history. Still, it's equally important to stay up to date with trends because, more than ever, the marketing landscape is constantly evolving. By staying informed and adapting to new trends, marketers can remain relevant, anticipate shifts in consumer preferences, and leverage innovative strategies and tools to effectively engage their target audience. As of today, here's an overview of the largest long-term trends that will likely impact marketing over the next few years.

- **Personalisation:** Consumers now expect personalised experiences and tailored messaging. Marketers leverage data analytics and technology to gather customer insights and deliver personalised content, offers, and recommendations across various channels.

- **Influencer Marketing:** Influencer marketing continues to grow in popularity. Marketers collaborate with social media influencers and content creators to promote their products or services, leveraging their credibility and large following to reach and engage target audiences.

- **Video Marketing:** Video content thrives across platforms such as YouTube, TikTok, Instagram and Snapchat. Marketers are using video marketing to capture attention, tell compelling stories, demonstrate products, and engage audiences in more immersive and dynamic ways.

- **Content Marketing:** Content marketing remains a prominent strategy for building brand authority, educating consumers, and driving engagement. Marketers focus on creating valuable, relevant, and high-quality content, including blog posts, articles, videos, podcasts, and social media posts.

- **Social Media Advertising:** Social media platforms continue to be key advertising channels. Marketers utilise paid social media advertising to reach specific target audiences; promote products or services; and drive website traffic, conversions, and brand awareness.

- **Voice Search Optimization:** With the rise of voice assistants like Amazon Alexa, Google Assistant, and Siri, optimizing content for voice search is gaining importance. Marketers optimise their websites and content to align with voice-based queries and provide concise and conversational answers.

- **User-Generated Content (UGC):** UGC involves leveraging consumer content, such as reviews, testimonials, and social media posts, to enhance brand credibility and authenticity. Marketers encourage customers to share their experiences and engage with UGC in their marketing strategies.

- **Sustainability and Purpose-Driven Marketing:** Consumers increasingly expect brands to align with sustainable practices and social causes. Marketers incorporate sustainability and purpose-driven initiatives into their brand messaging, highlighting environmental responsibility and social impact.

- **Augmented Reality (AR) and Virtual Reality (VR):** AR and VR technologies create immersive brand experiences. Marketers use AR/VR for virtual product trials, interactive brand storytelling, and engaging consumers in virtual environments.

- **Artificial Intelligence (AI) and Chatbots:** AI-powered tools and chatbots are being employed to automate customer interactions, provide personalised recommendations, and improve customer service. Marketers leverage AI to analyse data, automate ad targeting, and enhance overall marketing efficiency.

- **Data Privacy and Trust:** With growing concerns around data privacy, marketers are prioritising transparency, consent management, and secure data practices. Building trust with customers by protecting their data and respecting privacy is a key focus.

- **Mobile Marketing:** As mobile device usage continues to rise, mobile marketing is crucial. Marketers optimise websites for mobile devices, leverage mobile apps, and incorporate mobile-specific strategies such as location-based targeting and mobile advertising.

Marketing has come a long way, and using our power and influence ethically is more important than ever.

See also:

Marketing Fundamentals: Marketing Ethics
Marketing Communication: Influencer Marketing

Chapter 2

What is Marketing?

One may argue that marketing is perhaps the most misunderstood part of any business. While we are exposed to marketing every day, many people still do not understand what marketing truly is, what it involves, what it does not, and what consists of being a good marketer.

What is Marketing?

Marketing is a set of activities and processes used in businesses to promote and sell their products or services to consumers. The ultimate goal of marketing is to attract and retain customers, while making a profit for the business. As such, its mission is not too different from other functions like sales. Marketing involves creating and delivering a message to target audiences to influence their behaviour towards the offered product or service.

Marketing is a multi-faceted field with various sub-disciplines, each focusing on a different aspect of the marketing process, giving birth to the 'Marketing Umbrella' analogy. The marketing umbrella can be considered a metaphorical 'umbrella' that covers all aspects of marketing, such as advertising, public relations, sales promotions, direct marketing, personal selling, and digital marketing. Each of these elements can be considered spokes on the umbrella, with each contributing to the overall success of the marketing effort. Beautifully, marketing is always more significant than the sum of its parts.

As we work through the main ideas in marketing, one of the key components that will repeatedly come up is understanding the target audience. This means understanding their needs, preferences, and behaviours. Marketing is all about tailoring the product or message to resonate with the target audience, capture their attention, and prompt them to take action. Effective marketing campaigns leverage market research and data analytics insights to understand their audience better and create relevant messaging that speaks to their needs.

What Marketing is Not

The main confusion about what marketing is stems from the fact that most are only exposed to the result of effective marketing, for example, advertising. The reality is that 90% of marketing happens before the advert is shown on TV or that email reaches an inbox. So, before we get started, let's clear out some common misconceptions about marketing:

- **Marketing is not just advertising:** Advertising is a marketing component, not the only one. Marketing encompasses a range of activities beyond just advertising, including product development, market research, pricing, and distribution.

- **Marketing is not just sales:** Sales and Marketing are closely intertwined, but they are not the same. Sales focuses on selling a product or service to a customer, while marketing focuses on attracting and retaining customers through various tactics. The best salespeople deeply understand the customer, while the best marketers know how to sell their products well. Companies will always see the best results when both sales and marketing work hand in hand.

- **Marketing is not manipulation:** While marketing is designed to influence consumer behaviour, it is not about manipulation or deception. It is not about selling products or services people do not need or want. It is not about exploiting people's fears, insecurities, or vulnerabilities. Ethical marketing focuses on building trust and credibility with customers, rather than using deceptive tactics to make a sale. It's about amplifying existing preferences and communicating honestly, clearly, and respectfully with customers, enabling them to make informed decisions.

- **Marketing is not a one-size-fits-all approach:** Marketing strategies must be tailored to the specific needs and preferences of the target audience. There is no one-size-fits-all approach to marketing, and strategy must be adapted based on various factors, including product type, industry, and target market. This book will outline practical tools and frameworks that any business can adapt.

Why Marketing Matters

Marketing is critical for businesses of all sizes, as it is the primary means of attracting and retaining customers. Effective marketing campaigns can help businesses achieve various objectives, including:

- **Building brand awareness:** Marketing can help businesses raise awareness of their brand and differentiate themselves from competitors.

- **Increasing sales:** Marketing can drive sales by highlighting a product's or service's benefits and prompting customers to act.

- **Enhancing customer loyalty:** Marketing can help businesses build customer relationships by delivering a consistent and relevant message over time.

- **Generating leads:** Marketing campaigns can attract new customers and generate leads, providing a steady stream of potential customers for the business.

- **Supporting growth:** By understanding the needs and preferences of their target audience, businesses can develop new products and services that align with customer needs, supporting growth and expansion.

The Marketing Process

So, how does it work in practice? Marketing begins with identifying customer needs and wants to create a 'North Star' for the business. This requires a thorough understanding of the target market and its customers. Marketers use various techniques to gather information about customer needs and preferences, including surveys, focus groups, interviews, observation, and data analysis. They also monitor trends and changes in the market, such as technological advancements, demographic shifts, and economic conditions, to anticipate future demand and adjust their strategies accordingly.

Once marketers clearly understand customer needs and preferences, they develop offerings that satisfy them. This includes designing and developing products and services that are attractive, functional, and affordable, as well as creating marketing messages that resonate with the target audience. Next, they determine the appropriate pricing strategy based on factors such as the cost of production, competition, and perceived value.

Marketers use various promotional techniques to reach potential customers, such as advertising, sales promotion, personal selling, and public relations. These techniques generate awareness and interest in the product or service and persuade customers to purchase. The next step is to choose the appropriate distribution channels to make the product or service easily accessible to customers.

Finally, it's essential to monitor and evaluate the effectiveness of marketing strategies and make adjustments as needed. This step includes measuring the return on investment of various marketing activities, analysing customer feedback and satisfaction rates, and tracking sales and market share data.

When Marketing Goes Wrong

Dove is often heralded for its excellent marketing campaigns promoting natural beauty. However, this recent example shows how important it is to fully understand consumers and how even seasoned marketers get it wrong sometimes.

In 2017, Dove launched a new line of deodorants in China to expand its market share. The new deodorant line was marketed as gentle and moisturising and targeted women concerned about the harshness of traditional deodorants. Despite the success of Dove's other products in China, the deodorant launch failed to gain traction.

- **Cultural differences:** Chinese consumers have different preferences for personal care products, and Dove's marketing approach did not resonate with the local audience. In particular, using deodorants was not as widely accepted in China as in Western countries, which made it difficult for Dove to create a strong demand for its products.

- **Distribution:** Dove's deodorant line was not widely available in retail stores, and many consumers were not aware of the product's availability. This limited distribution made it difficult for Dove to generate awareness and build product demand.

- **Price:** Dove's deodorants were priced higher than other competitors in the Chinese market, making them less attractive to price-sensitive consumers. Many consumers were unwilling to pay a premium for a product they did not see offering additional benefits.

- **Brand perception:** Dove had previously faced criticism in China for an advertisement that was seen as insensitive and racist. This negative perception of the brand may have contributed to Chinese consumers' lack of interest in Dove's deodorants.

Ultimately, Dove's deodorant launch in China failed due to various factors. Despite the success of its other products in the country, the deodorant line could not gain traction and was eventually withdrawn from the market. This failure highlights the importance of understanding local market dynamics and tailoring products and marketing approaches to local preferences and cultural nuances.

While we don't dive into international marketing in particular in this book, all strategies and tools can be used across various markets. Whether for a single or multi-market campaign, an in-depth understanding of the local customer should remain any marketer's number one priority to deliver on the campaign's objectives.

What makes a good marketer?

Good marketers start from the premise that they know nothing. They possess a strong desire to gain insights and immerse themselves to genuinely comprehend the needs, attitudes, and behaviours of consumers. They acknowledge that their own perspectives are subjective and can be misleading, as they do not represent the entire consumer base.

Depending on the business size, marketing is one of the many hats a small business owner wears, or it can be a central part of the organisation with hundreds of people. Nevertheless, no matter what business, it's essential to understand that marketing requires a particular skill set to succeed.

Here are some critical skills that a good marketer should have:

- **Strategic Thinking:** A good marketer must be able to think strategically and develop marketing plans that align with the organisation's goals and objectives. They must be able to identify target audiences, understand their needs, and develop strategies to reach and engage them effectively.

- **Analytical Skills:** A good marketer must analyse market trends, customer behaviour, and data to create effective marketing strategies. They should be comfortable working with data, using analytical tools to track campaign performance, and making data-driven decisions.

- **Creativity:** A good marketer must be creative and innovative in their approach to marketing. They must be able to develop unique and engaging campaigns that capture the attention of their target audience and stand out from the competition.

- **Communication Skills:** A good marketer must have excellent communication skills to create compelling marketing messages that resonate with their target audience. They must articulate the benefits of their products or services in a way that potential customers quickly understand.

- **Time Management:** Good marketers must manage their time effectively to meet project deadlines and deliver timely marketing campaigns. They should be organised, prioritise tasks, and manage multiple projects simultaneously.

- **Sales Skills:** A good marketer should have a basic understanding of sales principles and be able to collaborate with sales teams to generate leads, close deals, and drive revenue growth. A natural rivalry is often suggested between both departments, but both work best when they work together.

Marketing is essential for companies to grow.

See also:

Brand Building: Marketing & Branding
Marketing Mix: The 6 P Framework
Consumer Behaviour: Behavioural Psychology in Marketing
Marketing Communication: Marketing & Advertising
Marketing Measurement: Decide > Commit > Measure > Repeat

Chapter 3

Marketing Ethics

It's far from the truth that marketers try brainwashing consumers to buy products. However, it is true that Marketers have a significant influence on society. As such, making ethical decisions is central to our jobs. If we can promote positive social impact by supporting social causes, advocating for diversity and inclusion, and avoiding harmful or offensive content, it is our responsibility to do so. Today's generation of consumers demands from companies to embrace ethical marketing, contribute to society's betterment, and be responsible corporate citizens.

While most companies adhere to ethical marketing practices, there have been instances of unethical conduct that have garnered attention:

- **Deceptive Advertising:** Various cases of deceptive advertising have occurred, where companies make false or misleading claims about their products or services to attract customers. Such practices mislead consumers, erode trust, and can result in legal consequences.

- **Privacy Breaches:** Incidents involving the mishandling of consumer data and privacy breaches have raised ethical concerns. Data breaches, unauthorised sharing of personal information, or unethical use of data for targeting purposes have harmed consumer trust and sparked debates on data privacy and protection.

- **Greenwashing:** The term refers to misleading claims about a product or company's environmental impact to create a false impression of environmental responsibility. Companies have faced criticism for exaggerating their eco-friendly practices while not making substantial efforts to minimise their environmental footprint.

- **Targeting Vulnerable Audiences:** Marketing tactics that exploit vulnerable populations, such as children or individuals with limited decision-making capacity, have drawn ethical scrutiny. Unethical targeting practices can manipulate vulnerable individuals into making choices that are not in their best interest.

- **Influencer Marketing Misconduct**: Instances of influencer marketing misconduct have emerged, including undisclosed sponsorships, fake reviews, and misleading endorsements. Such practices undermine trust in both the influencers and the brands they promote.

The road to hell is paved with good intentions, and from my experience, bad marketing is often a result of inexperience, lack of diversity among decision-makers, decisions made by the many, and narrow thought bubbles that cultivate the illusion of general acceptance. When working on any marketing project, it's worth keeping the following elements in mind to avoid missteps.

One central aspect of marketing ethics is the obligation to be **truthful and transparent** in all marketing communications. Marketers should avoid deceptive tactics, false claims, and misleading information that could potentially harm consumers or manipulate their purchasing decisions.

The collection, storage, and use of **consumer data** raise ethical concerns. Marketers should handle personal information responsibly, respecting consumer privacy rights, and ensuring data security. Transparent data policies and obtaining informed consent are crucial in maintaining ethical practices.

The **ethical implications of targeting certain demographic groups**, particularly vulnerable populations such as children, require careful consideration. Marketers should be mindful of potential harm, exploitation, or manipulation when designing marketing strategies aimed at these groups.

Marketing ethics also encompass a company's commitment to **social responsibility**, which involves considering the broader impact of marketing activities on society and the environment. Ethical marketing practices promote sustainability, support social causes, and avoid engaging in activities that can harm communities or the environment.

In addition, the rise of **influencer marketing** has also introduced new ethical challenges. Marketers should ensure transparency in sponsored content, clearly disclosing any financial relationships or incentives between influencers and brands. Authenticity and honesty in influencer endorsements are vital to maintain trust with the audience.

Pricing strategies that exploit consumer vulnerabilities or engage in price discrimination can raise ethical concerns. Marketers should strive for fairness, avoiding price gouging, hidden fees, or manipulative pricing tactics that take advantage of consumer information asymmetry.

Ethical marketing involves respecting cultural differences, avoiding offensive stereotypes, and **promoting diversity and inclusion.**

Marketers should be mindful of cultural contexts and ensure their campaigns are sensitive and respectful to different audiences.

The ethical implications of marketing extend to **environmental sustainability**. Marketers should consider the environmental impact of their products, packaging, and promotional activities. Green marketing practices, reducing waste, and promoting eco-friendly alternatives are essential for ethical marketing.

Intellectual property rights are crucial in marketing ethics. Marketers should not engage in plagiarism, unauthorised use of copyrighted material, or deceptive practices that infringe upon the intellectual property rights of others.

The foundation to all of the above, is a strong **ethical leadership and an organisational culture** prioritising ethical decision-making. Companies should establish clear ethical guidelines, provide training and support, and encourage a culture of integrity throughout their marketing teams.

The responsibility marketers bear towards society should not be taken lightly. The action of a few reflects on our profession as a whole.

See also:

Marketing Fundamentals: Marketing Ethics
Market Analysis: Consumer Profiling
Marketing Mix: Pricing
Marketing Communication: Marketing & Advertising
Marketing Communication: Influencer Marketing

Chapter 4

Marketing Budgets

Marketing budgets play a pivotal role in driving business growth and gaining a competitive edge. Setting a budget is notoriously difficult, even more so amidst economic uncertainty and the looming spectre of a recession.

An important point to understand is that Marketing should not be perceived solely as a cost centre but rather as a strategic investment for businesses. While marketing activities require financial resources, viewing them as mere expenses overlooks their potential to generate substantial returns. Effective marketing drives brand awareness, customer acquisition, and customer loyalty, resulting in increased sales and revenue growth. By investing in marketing initiatives, businesses can gain a competitive advantage, penetrate new markets, and build long-term relationships with customers. Moreover, marketing investments contribute to brand equity, positioning the business for sustained success and market differentiation. Recognising marketing as an investment empowers businesses to allocate resources strategically, measure ROI, and unlock the full potential of their marketing efforts.

Setting a Marketing Budget

In a world, where businesses often have a wide range of choices to make, setting a marketing budget is of paramount importance for businesses to effectively plan, execute, and measure their marketing efforts. With limited financial resources and ever-increasing competition, a well-defined budget provides a roadmap for allocating funds strategically across various marketing channels and initiatives. It allows businesses to prioritise their marketing activities based on their goals, target audience, and industry dynamics. A carefully planned budget ensures that resources are optimally allocated, preventing overspending or underspending on marketing activities. Moreover, a budget provides a foundation for accountability and measurement, enabling businesses to track the return on investment (ROI) and evaluate the effectiveness of their marketing strategies. Inspired by Marketing Expert Mark Ritson, the following 3-step approach aims to assist in setting budgets that deliver optimal results and maximise return on investment (ROI).

Step 1: Determining the Budget Size

Before embarking on any budget allocation, it is crucial for marketers to ascertain the appropriate financial resources required to fuel growth and secure a favourable market position. To aid in this process, a rule of thumb proposed by econometricians recommends spending between 5% and 10% of turnover on advertising to achieve the highest ROI.

Aiming for 10% of the business's turnover is likely to yield maximum efficiency and effectiveness, resulting in a competitive advantage. By adhering to this initial step, marketers can lay a strong foundation for their budget-setting process.

Step 2: Optimising the Allocation

Once the budget size has been determined, marketers must consider the balance between long-term brand building and short-term performance or activation. Both aspects are crucial for sustainable growth, as the brand sets the stage for sales, while activation or performance marketing drives the actual conversion. Finding the optimal ratio between the two is key to achieving success.

Research suggests that, on average, B2C brands should allocate 62% of their budget to brand building and 38% to activation. For B2B brands, the balance shifts slightly, with 46% allocated to brand building and 54% to activation. However, it is important to note that the optimal mix varies across different categories. For instance, financial services require an 80% emphasis on brand building, whereas retail benefits from a 64% focus on brand, and FMCG thrives with a 60% emphasis.

Despite the evidence supporting the benefits of brand investment, many businesses fail to allocate sufficient resources to this critical area. Companies often find themselves trapped in a short-term results-driven cycle. While investing heavily in short-term performance marketing may yield immediate ROI, it is essential to recognise that long-term brand building cannot be measured solely by short-term financial returns. Failing to allocate adequate funds to brand building can result in substantial revenue loss over time.

To optimise the allocation between brand building and performance marketing, marketers must understand their specific business requirements. Factors such as category, brand age, and the proportion of online and offline presence play a role in determining the ideal allocation. By aligning the budget allocation with these considerations, marketers can achieve a more effective and balanced approach.

Step 3: Measuring Success Appropriately

The final step in setting an effective marketing budget involves measuring the outcomes of both long-term brand building and short-term performance marketing, employing different metrics for each.

While return on investment (ROI) is a suitable metric for evaluating the effectiveness of short-term performance marketing, it is essential to move away from attempting to measure the ROI of long-term brand spend. Instead, trust should be placed in branding metrics that accurately gauge the impact and success of long-term brand strategies.

Recent surveys indicate a growing emphasis on tracking ROI, with many marketers acknowledging its importance to CEOs, CFOs, and board members. However, it is essential to recognise the limitations of ROI when evaluating brand building. Investing in branding initiatives may not yield immediate financial returns, but the impact can be significant in the long run. By focusing on branding metrics that capture brand perception, awareness, and loyalty, marketers can effectively measure the success of their brand-building efforts.

Managing Objections

Setting marketing budgets can be a challenging task for marketers, often accompanied by objections and scrutiny from stakeholders. This is primarily due to several factors that contribute to the complexity of budgeting decisions. Limited financial resources, uncertainties surrounding the effectiveness of marketing efforts, and the need to align marketing activities with broader business goals are common reasons for objections. Additionally, concerns about measuring return on investment (ROI) and external market factors further contribute to the objections faced by marketers. Understanding these challenges and effectively addressing them is essential for marketers to gain support and secure optimal budgets that drive business growth and success.

Limited Financial Resources

Objection: The objection may arise when the organisation has limited funds and believes that marketing budgets are an unnecessary expense or that the allocated budget is too high.

Resolution: Present a compelling business case for marketing investment by showcasing the potential return on investment (ROI) and the impact on business growth. Provide data-backed examples of successful marketing campaigns or industry benchmarks to demonstrate the effectiveness of marketing in achieving business objectives. Additionally, consider exploring alternative, cost-effective marketing strategies such as digital marketing, content marketing, or targeted campaigns to optimise the available resources.

Uncertainty about Marketing Effectiveness

Objection: Some stakeholders may question the effectiveness of marketing efforts, especially if they perceive marketing as intangible or difficult to measure in terms of outcomes.

Resolution: Provide evidence-based insights and data to demonstrate the impact of marketing on key performance indicators (KPIs) such as sales, customer acquisition, brand awareness, or customer satisfaction. Utilise marketing analytics, market research, and case studies to show the correlation between marketing activities and desired outcomes. Implement tracking mechanisms and performance measurement tools to monitor and report on the effectiveness of marketing initiatives, thereby addressing the concern about accountability and tangible results.

Lack of Alignment with Business Goals

Objection: Stakeholders may argue that marketing budgets are not aligned with the overall business goals or that marketing strategies are disconnected from other departments.

Resolution: Develop a clear and comprehensive marketing plan that aligns with the organisation's broader objectives. Highlight how marketing activities support sales, revenue growth, market share expansion, or customer engagement. Foster collaboration and communication between marketing and other departments to ensure that marketing initiatives are integrated with overall business strategies. Engage stakeholders in the budgeting process by seeking their input and addressing their concerns to create a sense of ownership and alignment.

Inadequate Measurement and ROI Assessment

Objection: Some stakeholders may question the ability to measure the return on marketing investment accurately, making it challenging to justify budget allocations.

Resolution: Implement robust measurement and analytics frameworks to track the performance and impact of marketing activities. Utilise key metrics, such as customer acquisition cost (CAC), customer lifetime value (CLV), conversion rates, or brand equity, to evaluate ROI and demonstrate the value generated by marketing efforts. Regularly review and report on the performance of marketing campaigns, providing insights on what worked, what didn't, and actionable recommendations for improvement. Transparently communicate the methodologies and metrics used for ROI assessment to instil confidence and trust in the budgeting process.

External Market Factors

Objection: External market factors, such as economic downturns or competitive pressures, may lead to objections about the effectiveness of marketing budgets during uncertain times.

Resolution: Conduct thorough market research and competitive analysis to understand market dynamics and consumer behaviour. Develop contingency plans and adapt marketing strategies based on changing market conditions. Emphasise the importance of maintaining brand presence and customer engagement during challenging times as an opportunity to gain market share or build resilience. Demonstrate how marketing can drive differentiation, customer loyalty, and brand reputation even in difficult economic circumstances.

Well thought out budgets drive focus and accountability, which in turn leads to more effective marketing overall.

See also:

Marketing Measurement: Data Analysis
Marketing Measurement: Key Performance Indicators
Marketing Measurement: The Balanced Scorecard

II

Market Analysis

Chapter 5

The SWOT Framework

The SWOT concept is a well-used framework to assess the firm's capabilities before starting or entering a market. As businesses have limited resources and need to use those finite resources to achieve their objectives, this analysis helps identify the internal and external factors that could pose challenges in executing the strategies.

In the context of marketing, a brand needs to identify its strong and weak suits to help determine which areas of a marketing campaign are working fine and which issues need to be addressed. Additionally, it helps determine the opportunities and threats in the external environment. The brand could use the opportunity to gain an advantage in the market. For instance, it can use that information to introduce a new product that fits the recent market trend. As for threats, early identification would help the brand develop solutions in the planning stage.

SWOT analyses are often showcased in a 4-box matrix. The top half focuses on internal factors—strengths and weaknesses—while the bottom half focuses on external factors: opportunities and threats. In addition, the left side (strengths and opportunities) focuses on the positives, while the right (weaknesses and threats) focuses on the negatives.

Strengths (S) – The first internal factor is strength. It helps businesses identify the operations and processes that are working well. The company could use these strengths to build a competitive advantage in the market. Marketers could use these strengths in their marketing strategies and influence the choices of their target audience.

Weaknesses (W) – The second internal factor is weakness. Managers could identify the areas that are not working optimally and improve them. It helps a business strengthen its position in the market. Marketers can use this factor to enhance marketing campaigns and provide better solutions to their target audience.

Opportunities (O) – The first external factor is opportunity. This factor helps a business to identify market opportunities and seize them effectively. When a company can identify an opportunity before its competitors, it gives it a head-start in taking advantage of the situation. Marketers use these opportunities to improve marketing campaigns and plan better strategies.

Threats (T) – The second external factor is a threat. It helps a business identify the problems and challenges in the market. A business can prepare itself better for these challenges through SWOT analysis. Marketers also use this factor to develop solutions for existing problems and challenges.

How to Create A SWOT

To conduct a SWOT analysis, businesses should ask themselves some of the following questions:

Strengths

- What are our unique selling points?
- What advantages do we have over our competitors?
- What skills and expertise do our employees possess?
- What resources do we have available, such as technology or financial capital?

- What positive feedback have we received from customers or clients?
- What products are performing well?

Weaknesses

- What are the areas we need to improve on?
- What are the limitations or constraints of our business?
- What skills or expertise do we lack?
- What feedback have we received from customers or clients that we need to address?
- What are our financial limitations?
- What products are underperforming?

Opportunities

- What emerging trends or changes in the market can we capitalise on?
- Are there any gaps in the market that we can fill?
- Are there any untapped customer segments that we can target?
- Can we expand our product or service offerings to attract new customers?
- Can we take advantage of new technologies or platforms to improve our business?

Threats

- Who are our competitors, and what are their strengths?
- Are there any market trends that can negatively affect our business?
- Are there any changes in regulations or laws that may impact our business?

- Are there any supply chain issues that may disrupt our business operations?
- What are the potential negative feedback from customers or clients we need to address?
- How are consumer trends changing?

Example of SWOT

Joe's Coffee Shop is a local coffee shop that has been in business for two years. They specialise in artisanal coffee and pastries and have a loyal customer base. However, they are facing some challenges and want to conduct a SWOT analysis to better understand their strengths, weaknesses, opportunities, and threats.

Strengths

- High-quality coffee and pastries made with locally sourced ingredients.
- A loyal customer base that appreciates the personalised service and friendly atmosphere.
- Prime location in a busy commercial area with high foot traffic.
- Unique decor and ambience set them apart from other coffee shops.

Weaknesses

- Limited menu options may not cater to the diverse tastes of all customers.
- Limited seating capacity may discourage customers from staying and socialising.
- Lack of an online ordering system may limit the convenience for customers.

- Limited marketing and advertising efforts that may not reach a broader audience.

Opportunities

- Expanding the menu to include more food options and catering to dietary restrictions and preferences.
- Investing in more comfortable seating arrangements and creating a more welcoming environment for customers.
- Introducing an online ordering and delivery system to reach customers who prefer to order from home or the office.
- Increasing marketing and advertising through social media, local events, and collaborations with other local businesses.

Threats

- Competition from other local and large chain coffee shops.
- Economic downturns or recessions may impact consumer spending on luxury items like speciality coffee and pastries.
- Consumer preferences and trends may shift towards healthier or more sustainable food options.
- Regulatory changes or health concerns may impact the supply chain of locally sourced ingredients.

By conducting a regular SWOT analysis, Joe's Coffee Shop can adapt to market trends, customer preferences, and regulatory changes to stay competitive and successful.

Criticism of the SWOT Model

SWOT is only one stage of business planning. Depending on the topic, it may contribute to the planning process. But relying wholeheartedly on it isn't advised.

Unfortunately, a SWOT analysis only concentrates on four primary factors. So, it only acts as a starting point for making informed business decisions.

One of the key things to watch out for is the lack of hierarchy. Which section needs attention first? Which one needs it the least?

The rigid structure might lead to poor decision-making. In SWOT analysis, businesses are expected to categorise attributes in only one of the four categories. There is no overlap. Once something is defined as a weakness, it can never be placed in the other three categories. A strength is a strength, never a weakness. An opportunity can never be a threat.

Such a black-and-white approach will lead to problems as the real world doesn't follow strict rules or guidance. A person can be charismatic but also a con artist. A business can have never-ending customers yet still sit in a financial hole. Nothing is ever just one thing. Businesses should think of SWOT analysis similarly.

SWOT is a tool to analyse the market before entering it.

See also:

Market Analysis: Insights
Marketing Measurement: Data Analysis

Chapter 6

The PESTLE Framework

The popular second step, following the SWOT, is an external PESTLE framework analysis. The external environment is important to the overall strategy, as today's ever-changing external factors can considerably impact the business's internal processes.

PESTLE analysis is an acronym for Political, Economic, Social, Technological, Legal, and Environmental factors. This chapter will discuss the importance of PESTLE analysis in marketing, its components, and its limitations.

Importance of PESTLE Analysis in Marketing:

- **Identify Market Opportunities:** This includes, for example, social trends or technological advancements can create new opportunities for companies to develop new products or services.

- **Understand Market Trends:** By analysing the external environment, companies can gain insight into and predict future market trends. This information is vital in developing strategies that align with market trends.

- **Mitigate Risks:** For example, changes in government policies or economic instability can affect the company's operations negatively. By understanding these risks, companies can develop contingency plans to mitigate the risks.

- **Develop Competitive Strategies:** PESTLE analysis helps companies understand their competitors and strategies. By analysing the external environment, companies can identify the strengths and weaknesses of their competitors and develop strategies to gain a competitive advantage.

- **Align with the Macro Environment:** For example, companies can develop environmentally friendly products that align with the macro environment if there is a shift towards sustainable products. Another example is the emphasis on corporate social responsibility. The legal and environmental aspects of the analysis allow businesses to review their policies considering this.

Components of the PESTLE Analysis

The PESTLE analysis consists of six components, each representing a different aspect of the external environment that can impact a company's operations.

1. **Political Factors:** This includes factors related to government policies, such as tax policies, trade restrictions, and regulations. Political factors can impact a company's operations by influencing its access to resources, ability to expand into new markets, and cost structure.

   For example, changes in tax policies can impact a company's profitability by increasing its tax burden. Similarly, trade restrictions can limit a company's ability to import or export goods, while regulations can impose additional costs on companies that are not compliant.

2. **Economic Factors:** This component of the PESTLE analysis includes factors such as inflation rates, exchange rates, and economic growth. Economic factors can impact a company's operations by affecting its revenue, cost structure, and profitability.

   For example, high inflation rates can increase a company's cost of goods sold, while low economic growth can limit its revenue growth. Similarly, fluctuations in exchange rates can impact a company's profitability by affecting the cost of its imports and exports.

3. **Social Factors:** This part looks at demographics, lifestyle changes, and cultural norms. Social factors can impact a company's operations by influencing its target market, customer preferences, and brand image.

   For example, changes in demographics can impact a company's target market by shifting the age or gender distribution of its customers. Similarly, changes in cultural norms can impact a company's brand image by influencing how customers perceive its products or services.

4. **Technological Factors:** Here the analysis deals with technological advancements, such as automation, artificial intelligence, and the internet. Technological factors can impact a company's operations by changing how it produces and delivers products or services and creating new opportunities for innovation.

For example, advancements in automation can reduce a company's labour costs, while the Internet can create new channels for marketing and sales. Similarly, artificial intelligence can improve a company's customer service by providing personalised recommendations and support.

5. **Legal Factors:** This includes factors related to laws and regulations, such as employment laws, consumer protection laws, and intellectual property laws. Legal factors can impact a company's operations by imposing additional costs, limiting its ability to expand into new markets, and creating legal liabilities.

For example, employment laws can impose additional costs on companies that are not compliant, while consumer protection laws can limit a company's ability to market and sell its products. Similarly, intellectual property laws can create legal liabilities for violating companies.

6. **Environmental Factors:** This component includes aspects, such as climate change, pollution, and resource depletion. Environmental factors can impact a company's operations by creating new risks and opportunities and influencing customer preferences and brand image.

For example, climate change can create risks for companies that rely on natural resources, while pollution can create reputational risks for companies perceived as being environmentally unfriendly. Similarly, resource depletion can create opportunities for companies to develop sustainable products.

Limitations of the PESTLE Analysis

While the PESTLE analysis is a valuable tool for companies to gain insight into the external factors that impact their business, it also has several limitations. These limitations include:

- **Lack of Specificity:** The analysis is a broad framework covering many factors. However, it does not provide specific guidance on addressing these factors or how they may impact the company.

- **Overemphasis on External Factors:** It's possible to overlook internal factors that can impact the company's operations. As a result, PESTLE may not provide a complete picture of the company's competitive position.

- **Limited Predictive Ability:** The framework provides a snapshot of the external environment at a particular time and may not accurately predict future trends and developments.

- **Interpretation Bias:** Like many analytical tools, PESTLE is subjective and open to interpretation, which can lead to bias and inaccurate conclusions.

PESTLE is a tool for external factors affecting business decisions.

See also:

Market Analysis: The SWOT Framework
Market Analysis: Insights
Marketing Measurement: Data Analysis

Chapter 7

Porter's 5 Forces

A Porter 5 forces analysis is a framework for assessing the competitive environment of a business industry. It is named after Michael E. Porter, a renowned strategy expert and Harvard Professor. It consists of five factors that determine the level of competition in an industry and affect a company's ability to generate profit. By using this model, businesses can understand the competitive forces in their industry and formulate strategies to stay competitive.

Porter's 5 Forces are the threat of new entrants, the bargaining power of suppliers, the bargaining power of buyers, the threat of substitutes, and the intensity of competitive rivalry. The analysis can be useful for businesses in various situations, including:

1. **Entering a new market:** A Porter 5 forces analysis can identify the key players, the competition level, and the entry barriers to a new market.

2. **Assessing the attractiveness of an industry:** Through this framework businesses can determine the attractiveness of an industry, such as the potential for profitability and growth.

3. **Evaluating competitive position:** By looking at the different factors, businesses can identify strengths and weaknesses in their business model and help them develop strategies to improve their position.

The 5 Forces Model

For large businesses, conducting this analysis is usually a formalised process; however, the framework can also be helpful for small to medium businesses as they set up their business plan and understand the viability of their new product in existing markets.

Let's dive into an overview of Porter's Five Forces model and explain each factor in detail with examples.

1. **Threat of new entrants:** This refers to the likelihood of new competitors entering the market and increasing competition. The threat of new entrants is higher when barriers to entry are low. For example, if it is easy and inexpensive to start a new business in an industry.

   One example of a high threat of new entrants in the retail industry. It is relatively easy to create a new retail business, and there are low barriers to entry. As a result, many small retail stores and online retailers compete with established retailers like Walmart and Amazon.

2. **Bargaining power of suppliers:** This factor deals with the suppliers' power over the price of raw materials or other inputs. The bargaining power of suppliers is higher when there are few suppliers and when the supplier's products are critical to the company's operations.

   One example of the high bargaining power of suppliers is the automotive industry. The manufacturers rely on a few large suppliers for essential parts like engines and transmissions.

The suppliers have significant bargaining power because they are the only sources of these critical parts.

3. **Bargaining power of buyers:** The third force in Porter's Five Forces is the bargaining power of buyers. This refers to buyers' power over the price and quality of a company's products or services. The bargaining power of buyers is higher when they have many options to choose from and when the company's products or services are not unique.

   One example of the high bargaining power of buyers is the airline industry. Consumers have many different airlines to choose from, and the airlines' products are not significantly different. As a result, airlines must compete on price and other factors like customer service to attract customers.

4. **Threat of substitutes:** This factor assesses the likelihood of customers switching to a substitute product or service. The threat of substitutes is higher when many substitute products or services are available and comparable in quality.

   One example of a high threat of substitutes is the soft drink industry. There are many different brands of soft drinks, and they are all very similar in taste and quality. As a result, consumers can easily switch between brands without significant consequences.

5. **Intensity of competitive rivalry:** The final force is the intensity of competitive rivalry. This refers to the level of competition between existing companies in an industry. The

intensity of competitive rivalry is higher when there are many competitors, and they are all similarly sized.

One example of high-intensity competitive rivalry is the fast-food industry. Many different fast-food restaurants offer similar products at similar prices. As a result, they must compete fiercely to attract customers and generate profits.

The level of data needed to conduct a viable Porter's 5 forces analysis can seem daunting. As with all frameworks, the results of an analysis are only as good as the raw data fed into the process. Here are some starting points on where relevant information can be found:

- **Industry structure:** Gather information about the size of the industry, the number of players, and the market share of the leading players.

- **Competitive rivalry:** Analyse the intensity of competition in the industry, including the pricing strategies, marketing efforts, and product differentiation versus competitors.

- **Bargaining power of suppliers:** Gather information about the number of suppliers, the availability of substitutes, and the level of control suppliers have over prices and quality.

- **Bargaining power of buyers:** Analyse the bargaining power of customers, including their purchasing volume, the availability of alternatives, and the level of control over prices.

- **Threat of substitutes:** Gather data on substitutes' availability, price and quality, and the likelihood of customers switching to them.

Marketers can collect data from various sources, such as government statistics, industry reports, market research firms, trade associations, and online databases. Some valuable sources for data include:

- **Bureau of Labour Statistics (BLS):** Provides data on industries and market trends.

- **IBISWorld:** A market research firm that provides comprehensive industry reports and analysis.

- **Local trade associations:** Industry-specific organisations that provide data, insights, and networking opportunities for businesses.

- **Market research firms:** Companies specialising in collecting and analysing market data and trends.

- **Online databases:** Resources such as Statista, Data.gov, and Euromonitor provide access to industry statistics, market reports, and other data sources.

Limitations of the Model

As with all models, it's important to understand the limitations of the Porter model.

- **Limited Scope:** Porter's Five Forces model only focuses on analysing an industry's competitive environment. It doesn't consider other important factors affecting a company's performance, such as technology, innovation, and globalisation.

- **Static Analysis:** The model assumes that the industry's competitive forces are relatively stable, and that the company's strategy is unlikely to change. However, competitive forces can change rapidly in today's fast-changing business environment, making the model less relevant.

- **Industry Definition:** The model's usefulness depends on how an industry is defined. The boundaries of an industry can be ambiguous, and the model may not apply to all industries.

- **Lack of Practical Guidance:** The model provides a theoretical framework but doesn't offer practical guidance on implementing the findings. Companies need more specific recommendations on how to deal with competitive forces.

- **Neglects External Factors:** Porter's Five Forces model ignores external factors such as political, economic, social, and technological forces, which can also affect the industry's competitiveness.

Porter's 5 forces provide a temperature check on how much competition a business will face in an industry.

See also:

Market Analysis: Bowman's Strategic Clock
Market Analysis: Insights
Marketing Measurement: Data

Chapter 8

Competition

Competition is a standard occurrence in all business environments and indicates a thriving market. Generally speaking, it increases market efficiency, encouraging firms to optimise their use of resources and strategy in ways that give them an advantage over competitors. Before discussing the types of competition in more detail, let's look at examples of why competition is important for any business environment:

- **Encourages innovation:** Competition drives businesses to develop new and better products or services to gain a competitive edge. That is because, in an ever-changing market, companies that stand still risk losing customers to their competitors. Therefore, the competition encourages businesses to improve their offerings to meet customers' changing needs on a continuous basis.

- **Lowers prices:** When businesses compete, they often lower their prices to attract more customers. This benefits consumers as they have more options and can purchase products or services at a lower price. In a competitive market, businesses are less likely to charge excessive prices because customers have other options.

- **Improves quality:** Other than just looking at the price, the competition encourages businesses to focus on product quality to differentiate themselves from competitors.

Businesses that provide high-quality products or services are more likely to attract and retain customers. Therefore, competition drives businesses to improve their quality standards to stay ahead.

- **Increases customer choice:** As previously mentioned, competition leads to a wider variety of products or services being available to customers. When businesses compete, they offer different features, styles, or price points to appeal to different customers. This gives customers more choices and enables them to select the product or service that best fits their needs and preferences.

- **Boosts economic growth:** Overall, competition drives innovation, productivity, and efficiency, which can lead to economic growth. Businesses are more likely to create jobs, invest in new technology and infrastructure, and contribute to economic growth. Therefore, competition is not only good for consumers but also for the economy as a whole.

Types of Competition

Marketing plays a vital role in a competitive landscape as it shapes how businesses operate, what products they offer, and how they market those products to their customers. Depending on the type of competition a business or product faces, the marketing strategies might differ.

Direct Competition

Direct competition occurs when two or more companies offer similar products or services to the same target market. These companies compete head-to-head for the same customers.

Examples of direct competition include McDonald's and Burger King, Coca-Cola and Pepsi, and Amazon and Walmart.

Indirect Competition

Indirect competition occurs when two or more companies offer different products or services that satisfy the same customer need. Although they do not offer the same products, they compete for the same customer dollars. For example, a restaurant may not directly compete with a grocery store, but both offer solutions for people who need to eat.

Substitute Competition

Substitute competition occurs when two or more companies offer different products or services that can be used as substitutes for each other. These products or services are not identical, but similar enough to be considered alternatives. For example, a consumer may substitute a bicycle for a car or a video game for a movie.

Monopolistic Competition

Monopolistic competition occurs when many companies offer similar but not identical products or services. They are differentiated based on quality, design, or brand features. Each company seeks to differentiate its products to gain a competitive advantage. Examples of monopolistic competition include Nike and Adidas in the athletic footwear market.

Oligopolistic Competition

Oligopolistic competition occurs when a few companies dominate a market. Each company has significant market power, and the actions of one company can affect the others. Companies may collaborate in this competition to set prices or limit competition. Examples of oligopolistic competition include the airline industry, where a few major carriers control most of the market.

Perfect Competition

Perfect competition is a hypothetical scenario that is extremely hard to find in reality. It occurs when many companies offer identical products or services to many buyers. Each company is a price taker, meaning it cannot influence the product's price. In this type of competition, companies cannot differentiate their products or services, and profits are driven to zero. The closest example to this would be the stock market; however, even there, competition is not fully perfect.

Global Competition

Global competition occurs when companies compete with each other in multiple countries around the world. In this type of competition, companies face diverse customers, cultures, and regulations. Companies must adapt their marketing strategies to suit each market they operate in. Examples of global competition include Coca-Cola, McDonald's, and Starbucks, all of which have a significant international presence.

Brand Competition

Brand competition happens when two or more companies offer the same product or service but have different brand images. It's an essential type of competition in marketing because consumers often make purchasing decisions based on brand loyalty, brand recognition, and brand reputation. Brands that offer more value, better customer service, and a more recognisable brand image have a competitive advantage.

For example, Coca-Cola and Pepsi are two companies that compete against each other in the soft drink industry. While both offer similar products, they have different brand images, marketing strategies, and target audiences.

David Versus Goliath

As barriers to entry are slowly getting democratised through automation, we're increasingly seeing small and medium businesses entering markets previously dominated by large players. Generally speaking, SMEs can successfully compete with larger businesses if they look at the following factors:

- **Focus on niche markets:** Small businesses can target a specific niche market that larger businesses may overlook. By catering to a specific group of customers, small businesses can establish themselves as experts in their field and build a loyal customer base.

- **Provide personalised service:** Small businesses can provide more personalised service to their customers than larger businesses. This can include customised products, individualised attention, and a more personal relationship with customers.

- **Emphasise quality:** Small businesses can emphasise the quality of their products or services over quantity.

- **Leverage technology:** Small businesses can leverage technology to compete with larger businesses. For example, they can use social media to reach a wider audience, use eCommerce platforms to sell their products online, and use cloud-based software to streamline their operations.

- **Collaborate with other businesses:** Small businesses can collaborate to increase their reach and resources. For example, they can partner with other small businesses to offer bundled products or services or partner with larger businesses to gain access to new markets.

- **Be agile and adaptable:** Small businesses are often more agile than larger ones. They can quickly pivot their strategy to respond to changing market conditions and customer needs.

- **Build a strong brand:** Small businesses can build a strong brand identity that resonates with their customers by developing a unique brand voice and visual identity.

One example of a small brand successfully entering a market dominated by large competitors is the case of Dollar Shave Club, a subscription-based service that delivers razors and other grooming products to customers on a monthly basis.

When Dollar Shave Club launched in 2011, the market for razors and grooming products was dominated by large competitors such as Gillette and Schick, who had established brand recognition and wide distribution networks. However, Dollar Shave Club competed by leveraging its strengths and addressing customers' pain points.

First, Dollar Shave Club developed a unique value proposition. They positioned themselves as a more affordable alternative to the high-priced razors sold by their larger competitors. They also focused on convenience, offering a subscription-based service that delivered razors and other grooming products directly to customers' homes.

Second, Dollar Shave Club developed a strong brand identity that resonated with its target audience. They used humour and irreverence to differentiate themselves from their competitors' more serious and conservative marketing strategies. This helped them build a loyal customer base and generate buzz on social media.

Third, Dollar Shave Club leveraged technology to streamline its operations and reach customers. They used an eCommerce platform to sell their products online and used data analytics to optimise their marketing campaigns and improve customer retention.

As a result of these strategies, Dollar Shave Club was able to gain market share quickly and compete with larger competitors. By 2016, the company had more than 3 million subscribers and had generated more than $200 million in revenue.

In 2016, Dollar Shave Club was acquired by Unilever for $1 billion. The acquisition was a testament to the success of the small brand's strategy and its ability to compete with large competitors in a highly competitive market.

Competition is a sign of a healthy market and benefits both consumers and businesses in the long term.

See also:

Market Analysis: The PESTLE Framework
Market Analysis: Bowman's Strategic Clock
Market Analysis: The Blue Ocean Strategy
Brand Building: Brand Positioning

Chapter 9

Bowman's Strategic Clock

Bowman's Strategic Clock is a model used to analyse a company's competitive position in the market. The model was developed by Cliff Bowman and David Faulkner in 1996 and is based on Porter's generic strategies. The Strategic Clock identifies eight different strategic positions that a company can take based on two dimensions: price and perceived value.

This model is a useful tool for businesses to assess their competitive position and to identify strategies to improve their market position. This section will explore the components of Bowman's Strategic Clock.

Components of Bowman's Strategic Clock

The Strategic Clock is based on two dimensions: price and perceived value. The price dimension measures the price of a product or service relative to the market average. The perceived value dimension measures how customers perceive the value of a product or service compared to its competitors.

The eight strategic positions in Bowman's Strategic Clock are:

1. **Low Price/Low Value:** This position is characterised by low prices and low perceived value. Companies in this position typically sell low-quality products or services and compete on price. This position is often referred to as the 'bargain basement' position.

2. **Low Price:** This position is characterised by low prices but relatively high perceived value. Companies in this position can offer lower prices due to their lower cost structure or economies of scale. Examples of companies in this position include Walmart and Southwest Airlines.

3. **Hybrid:** This position is characterised by medium prices and medium perceived value. Companies in this position offer a balance between price and quality. This position is often called the 'middle of the road' position.

4. **Differentiation:** This position is characterised by high prices and high perceived value. Companies in this position offer unique products or services that are difficult to imitate. Examples of companies in this position include Apple and Rolex.

5. **Focused Differentiation:** This position is similar to the Differentiation position, but it is focused on a specific market segment. Companies in this position offer unique products or services that are tailored to the needs of a specific group of customers. Examples of companies in this position include Tesla and Whole Foods.

6. **Increased Price/Low Value:** This position is characterised by high prices but low perceived value. Companies in this position are often able to charge higher prices due to brand recognition or customer loyalty. Still, their products or services are not necessarily higher quality than their competitors. This position is often referred to as the 'rip-off' position.

7. **Increased Price:** This position is characterised by high prices and medium perceived value. Companies in this position can charge higher prices due to a unique feature or

attributed to their products or services. Examples of companies in this position include Starbucks and Bose.

8. **Low Value:** This position is characterised by medium to high prices but low perceived value. Companies in this position are selling products or services that are not unique or differentiated from their competitors. This position is often referred to as the 'commodity' position.

Limitations of Bowman's Strategic Clock

While Bowman's Strategic Clock is a valuable tool for analysing a company's competitive position and identifying possible strategic options, it has limitations.

- **Overemphasis on price:** The clock places a lot of emphasis on price as a differentiator. While price is essential in many markets, it is not the only factor customers consider when purchasing. Factors like quality, convenience, and brand reputation can be just as important, if not more so, than price.

- **Limited focus on differentiation:** The clock does not provide a comprehensive framework for analysing differentiation strategies. While it identifies several generic strategies, such as focused differentiation and hybrid strategies, it does not guide how to achieve differentiation in practice. Companies may need to look beyond the clock to other frameworks, such as Porter's Five Forces, to develop effective differentiation strategies.

- **Ignores the impact of technology:** The clock was developed before the rise of the internet and digital technologies. As a result, it does not fully account for the impact of these technologies on markets and competition. In today's digital age, companies need to consider a range of digital strategies, such as online advertising and social media marketing, in addition to the traditional strategies identified by the clock.

- **May oversimplify complex markets:** The clock is designed to be a simple and accessible tool for analysing markets. However, this simplicity may result in an oversimplification of complex markets. In some markets, there may be many competitors, each with its unique strategy and competitive position.

- **Does not account for cultural differences:** The clock assumes a relatively homogeneous market regarding customer preferences and behaviour. However, in reality, markets can be very diverse, with customers in different regions and cultures having different preferences and behaviours. The clock may not fully account for these differences, and companies may need to tailor their strategies to specific markets and customer segments.

Despite these limitations, Bowman's Strategic Clock remains a valuable tool for companies looking to develop effective competitive strategies. By using the clock to analyse their competitive position and identify potential strategic options, companies can develop strategies tailored to their specific market to help them succeed in an increasingly competitive business environment.

Bowman's Strategic Clock is useful to identify a company's competitive position and possible strategic options.

See also:

Market Analysis: Porter's 5 Forces
Market Analyis: Competition
Brand Building: Brand Positioning
Marketing Mix: Price

Chapter 10

Consumer Profiling

Rather than making hasty assumptions, good marketing acknowledges the need to avoid over-generalisation and stereotyping. They recognize that each consumer is unique, with varying preferences, behaviours, and characteristics, and they approach their marketing strategies with a nuanced understanding of this diversity.

Humans are complex and diverse, so marketers seek to cluster certain consumer types to target them more effectively. Here we differentiate by two levels: segmentation and profile.

Customer segmentation divides a customer base into larger groups based on needs, preferences, and characteristics. Profiles are then developed, representing a more zoomed-in view. Imagine a dart board, with the board being the segment and the bullseye being the ideal consumer profile. While trying to hit the bullseye, the business is more likely to hit the wider dart board.

In this section, we will explore the difference between customers and consumers, look at how to identify a segment, and learn to write a profile through an example.

Benefits of Consumer Targeting

While creating segments and profiles can sometimes feel overly time-consuming, it's a cornerstone of effective marketing.

Charles, the Prince of Wales, and Ozzy Osbourne, sometimes called 'The Prince of Darkness', were both born in 1984. They are both wealthy and famous males who were raised in the UK, lived in a castle, and have been married twice. Yet, most people agree that Charles and Ozzy are very different personalities who would be receptive to different marketing messages.

- **Targeted marketing campaigns:** By segmenting customers into groups, businesses can create targeted marketing campaigns more likely to reach and resonate with each specific group. This results in more efficient use of marketing resources, as businesses can focus their efforts on the most promising segments.

- **Improved customer experience:** By understanding the unique needs of each customer group, businesses can provide a more personalised experience for each customer, leading to greater customer satisfaction and loyalty.

Consumer Versus Customer

The terms 'customer' and 'consumer' are often used interchangeably, but they have different meanings and implications for a business's marketing strategy. Understanding the difference between these terms is imperative in order for businesses to target and engage with their target audience effectively.

A customer refers to the person or entity who purchases a product or service from a business. This can include individuals, businesses, or organisations. Customers may make a one-time purchase or be repeat buyers and may have varying levels of loyalty to a particular brand or product.

A **consumer,** on the other hand, refers to the person who ultimately uses or consumes a product or service. This can be the same person as the customer, but it can also be a different individual. For example, a parent may be the customer who purchases toys for their children, but the children are the consumers who use and enjoy the toys.

Differentiating between customers and consumers is important because it allows businesses to tailor their messaging and strategies to each group. For example, a business may market a product to the customer based on features like price, convenience, or quality while focusing on the product's benefits and appeal to the consumer. By understanding their needs, preferences, and motivations, businesses can create more targeted and effective marketing campaigns that resonate with their target audience.

How to Create Segments

- **Demographic Segmentation:** This involves segmenting customers based on demographic characteristics such as age, gender, income, education level, and marital status. For example, a business selling baby products would likely target a different demographic than a business selling luxury cars.

- **Geographic Segmentation:** This involves segmenting customers based on their geographic location, country, region, city, or postcode. This is particularly relevant for businesses that operate in specific geographic areas, such as local retailers or service providers.

- **Behavioural Segmentation:** This involves segmenting customers based on their behaviour, such as their buying habits, brand loyalties, and online activities. For example, a business might segment customers based on purchase frequency, product preferences, or social media engagement.

- **Psychographic Segmentation:** This involves segmenting customers based on their personality traits, values, and interests. This type of segmentation is beneficial for businesses that sell products or services appealing to specific lifestyle segments, such as luxury goods, wellness products, or outdoor gear.

Once companies have identified customer segments, they must evaluate them to determine which segments are worth targeting. To do this, consider the following factors:

- **Size:** Is the segment large enough to be profitable?

- **Growth potential:** Is the segment likely to grow in the future?

- **Profitability:** Will targeting this segment be profitable?

- **Accessibility:** Can the segment be reached through marketing efforts?

- **Competitiveness:** How many competitors are targeting this segment?

Based on these factors, businesses can prioritise segments and decide which ones to target first.

How to Write a Consumer Profile

Once a company has segmented its customers, the next step is to create a consumer profile for each segment. A consumer profile describes the ideal customer for each segment, including their demographic information, preferences, and behaviours. Here are the steps to creating a consumer profile:

- **Define the segment:** Start by defining the specific segment to profile. This could be based on any of the segmentation criteria mentioned above.

- **Conduct research:** Conducting research to collect data about the target customer's preferences, behaviours, and characteristics. This can be done through surveys, interviews, focus groups, or other market research methods.

- **Identify key attributes:** Identifying the key attributes that define the target customer. These may include demographic characteristics such as age, gender, income, and education level, as well as behavioural traits such as buying habits, brand loyalty, and online activity.

- **Create a profile:** Companies create a detailed consumer profile for each segment using the information gathered in the research. This should include a description of the target customer's needs, preferences, behaviours, and demographic information.

Example of a Consumer Profile

After identifying and evaluating customer segments, marketers can create a consumer profile for each segment. A consumer profile is a detailed description of a business's ideal customer within a particular segment. Think of it like the bullseye on a dart board, representing the broader segment. It should include demographic information, psychographic information, and behavioural information. It's important to understand that the person described in the profile is a fictional character representing a group of people. But the more detailed the profile, the more targeted marketing campaigns can be developed.

Here is an example of a consumer profile for a local hardware shop:

Consumer Profile 1

Name: Tom
Age: 28
Gender: Male
Income: $45,000 per year

Psychographic: Tom is an adventurous person who enjoys hiking and outdoor activities. He has a positive attitude towards life and continually seeks new challenges. He is interested in sustainable living and likes incorporating eco-friendly products into daily life.

Behavioural: Tom is a regular customer at the local hardware shop. He enjoys purchasing outdoor equipment, such as camping gear and hiking tools. He prefers to shop in-store to see and touch the products before purchasing. Furthermore, he also follows the hardware shop on social media and is responsive to email marketing campaigns.

Communication: Tom prefers to communicate via email or social media. He follows the hardware shop on Instagram and Facebook, and he engages with their posts. He also responds well to marketing campaigns sent via email and enjoys receiving updates on new products or sales.

Consumer Profile 2

Name: Susan
Age: 42
Gender: Female
Income: $100,000 per year

Psychographic: Susan is a busy professional who values her time and enjoys being organised. She is interested in interior design and enjoys DIY projects around her home. She is passionate about sustainability and likes incorporating eco-friendly products into her lifestyle.

Behavioural: Susan is a regular customer at the local hardware shop. She enjoys purchasing home improvement products such as paint and hardware tools. She prefers to shop in-store to see the products in person before purchasing. Furthermore, she also follows the hardware shop on social media and subscribes to their newsletter for updates on new products and sales.

Communication: Susan prefers to communicate via email or in-store. She appreciates personalised attention and values the expertise of the hardware shop staff. She responds well to marketing campaigns sent via email and enjoys receiving updates on new products or sales.

Consumer segments allow companies to tailor marketing messages and product offerings to a specific group of people.

See also:

Market Analysis: Insights
Market Analysis: Marketing Research
Market Analysis: Bias in Research

Chapter 11

Insights

Marketing insights are valuable information from analysing consumer behaviour, market trends, and industry data. These insights can help businesses grow by identifying potential opportunities and threats and creating more effective marketing strategies. The term 'insight' has become a buzzword in the business world, so it is often overused and misinterpreted in the sense that basic data points are often deemed as 'insights'. However, to effectively use insights in business, it is important to understand what they are and how to identify them. Here we will explore marketing insights, how to find them, and how to use them in marketing strategy.

What are Marketing Insights?

Good marketers understand that insights are not about asking consumers what they want. Instead, they delve deeper by inquiring about actual experiences, actively listening, and observing to gain a fresh perspective. They extract genuine problems from the insights they gather and collaborate with a diverse team to develop solutions that customers prefer over alternatives. Moreover, these solutions should align with the company's capabilities, ensuring they can be effectively delivered in a way that is beneficial to both the customers and the business.

In essence, an insight is a deep understanding of customers' needs, desires, and motivations that goes beyond surface-level observations. Insights are not simply facts or data points; they are meaningful and actionable interpretations of customer behaviours and attitudes.

To identify an insight in business, one must go beyond superficial observations and look for patterns and underlying drivers of behaviour. This can be done through qualitative and quantitative research methods, such as surveys, focus groups, interviews, and observational studies.

An insight typically consists of several key features. First, it is rooted in customer behaviour or attitudes rather than internal company data or assumptions. Second, it is relevant and meaningful to the business, providing a clear path for action or improvement. Third, it is specific and actionable, providing a clear direction for decision-making.

To differentiate between an insight and a simple observation or data point, one must ask the following questions: What is the underlying motivation behind the behaviour or attitude? What is the customer trying to achieve or avoid? How does this insight inform business strategy or decision-making?

How to Find Marketing Insights

There are several ways to find marketing insights. Some of the most common methods include:

- **Conducting Market Research:** Market research is a systematic process of collecting and analysing data to understand the target markets. This can include surveys, focus groups, and in-depth interviews with customers. Market research allows businesses to gain valuable insights into customer needs, preferences, and behaviours.

- **Analysing Sales Data:** Sales data can provide insights into customer behaviours and preferences. This can include information such as which products are selling the most, which products are being returned the most, and which products are recommended by customers.

- **Monitoring Social Media:** Social media is a powerful tool for understanding customer sentiment and behaviours. This can include analysing customer reviews, comments, and social media interactions.

- **Analysing Website Traffic:** Analysing website traffic can provide insights into customer behaviours and preferences. This can include information such as which web pages are being visited the most, which pages are causing customers to leave the site, and which pages generate the most leads.

How to Use Marketing Insights in Marketing Strategy

Once a business has identified marketing insights, the next step is to use them to inform marketing strategy.

Step 1 Identify Target Audience: Use insights to create a consumer profile representing the target audience. This profile should include information such as demographic data, interests, and behaviours.

Step 2 Create Targeted Messaging: Use the insights gathered to create targeted messaging that resonates with the target audience. This messaging should be tailored to specific needs and preferences.

Step 3 Create Customised Offers: Use the insights gathered to create customised offers that appeal to the target audience. This can include creating targeted promotions, discounts, and loyalty programs.

Step 4 Optimise for Marketing Channels: Use the insights gathered to optimise the marketing channels. This can include identifying which channels are most effective at reaching the business target audience and allocating marketing budgets accordingly.

Step 5 Test and Iterate: Use the insights gathered to test and iterate the marketing strategy continually. This can include conducting A/B tests to determine which messaging and offers are most effective and to adjust the strategy accordingly.

Example of Using Marketing Insights in a Marketing Strategy

Let's say we're looking at a small business that sells organic skincare products. They have conducted market research and identified that their target audience is primarily women aged 25-45 who are interested in natural and organic products. They have also analysed sales data and identified that the best-selling products are facial moisturisers and body lotions.

Based on these insights, the business creates a consumer profile representing the target audience. This profile includes information such as age, gender, interests, and behaviours.

Next, they create targeted messaging that speaks directly to the target audience. This messaging emphasises the natural and organic ingredients in skin care products and the benefits they provide for the skin.

Marketing Insights in the Market

These examples can help illustrate the importance of properly identifying and utilising insights in marketing strategies.

Good Marketing Insights

Apple's 'Think Different' campaign: Apple's insight that their customers didn't want to be just consumers of technology, but innovators and creators, led to the development of their 'Think Different' campaign. This campaign resonated with its target audience and helped Apple become a leader in innovation and creativity in the technology industry.

Dove's 'Real Beauty'campaign: Dove's insight that women wanted to see real, diverse beauty in advertisements rather than unattainable standards led to their 'Real Beauty' campaign. This campaign not only resonated with their target audience but also sparked a larger societal conversation about beauty standards.

Coca-Cola's 'Share a Coke' campaign: Coca-Cola's insight that customers wanted a more personalised experience with their products led to the development of their 'Share a Coke' campaign. This campaign allowed customers to purchase personalised Coca-Cola bottles with their names on them, significantly increasing sales and customer engagement.

Bad Marketing Insights

Pepsi's 'Protest' advertisement: Pepsi's insight that young people wanted to be a part of social movements and activism led to their 'Protest' advertisement. However, the advertisement was criticised for trivialising important social issues and was ultimately pulled.

McDonald's 'Arch Deluxe' campaign: McDonald's insight that customers wanted a more sophisticated burger option led to the development of their 'Arch Deluxe' campaign. However, the campaign failed to resonate with its target audience and ultimately resulted in a loss of sales for the fast-food giant.

New Coke: Coca-Cola's insight that customers wanted a sweeter, smoother Coca-Cola led to the development of 'New Coke'. However, the new formula was widely disliked by customers, leading to a significant decrease in sales and, ultimately, the reintroduction of the original recipe as 'Coca-Cola Classic'.

These examples demonstrate the importance of conducting proper research and analysis to identify valuable insights for effective marketing strategies. A good marketing insight should be relevant to the target audience, resonate with them emotionally or intellectually, and be actionable within the context of the brand and its goals. A bad marketing insight, on the other hand, can lead to misguided campaigns that fail to resonate with customers and ultimately harm the brand's reputation and sales.

Good insights are data-driven and act as a north star for the business.

See also:

Market Analysis: Marketing Research
Market Analysis: Bias in Research
Marketing Measurement: Data Analysis

Chapter 12

Marketing Research

When discussing marketing, the first step is always understanding the customer. Marketing research is crucial for any business that wants to understand its customers, competitors, and market trends. It is a systematic approach to gathering, analysing, and interpreting information that can help a company make informed decisions about its marketing strategies. In this chapter, we will discuss marketing research, why it is necessary, the different types of research, and how small businesses can conduct marketing research.

What is Marketing Research?

Marketing research is the process of gathering, analysing, and interpreting data that can help a business make informed decisions about its marketing strategies. The data can come from various sources, including surveys, focus groups, observation, and secondary sources. Marketing research can help businesses identify market trends, customer needs and preferences, and competitive advantages and disadvantages.

Why is Marketing Research Important?

Marketing research provides companies with information to help them make informed decisions about their marketing strategies. By understanding customer needs and preferences, businesses can develop products and services that meet those needs and differentiate themselves from competitors. It can also help companies identify growth and expansion opportunities and avoid costly mistakes.

Different Types of Research

Data can be gathered from various sources. In marketing, we classify the two main types of sources into primary research and secondary research.

Primary Research: Primary research involves gathering data directly from customers or potential customers. Surveys, focus groups, and observations are primary research methods.

- **Surveys:** This is a popular method of primary research that involves asking a series of questions to a group of people. Generally, they can be conducted online, through the mail, or in person.

- **Focus Groups:** Focus groups involve bringing people together to discuss a product or service. The group is typically led by a moderator who asks questions and facilitates the discussion.

- **Observation:** Observation involves watching and recording the behaviour of customers or potential customers. This method is often used in retail settings or product testing.

Secondary Research: Secondary research involves gathering data from existing sources, such as industry reports, government publications, and company websites.

Within the primary and secondary research areas, we further differentiate if the type of data gathered is qualitative or quantitative. Each research type has unique characteristics, strengths, and weaknesses.

Qualitative research is exploratory research used to gain insights and understand people's behaviours, attitudes, opinions, and motivations. Qualitative research involves collecting and analysing data through non-numerical methods, such as interviews, focus groups, observation, and content analysis. It aims to identify themes, patterns, and trends in data that can provide insights into consumer behaviour or market trends. This type of research is beneficial when exploring new or emerging topics, when researchers have limited prior knowledge, or when the research focuses more on depth than breadth.

For example, a market researcher conducting a qualitative research project on consumer preferences for a new food product may conduct research with focus groups to understand their attitudes and behaviours towards the product. The researcher may ask participants open-ended questions and encourage discussion to uncover their motivations, opinions, and emotions about the product. The researcher will then analyse the data to identify key themes and trends in the participants' responses.

Quantitative research, on the other hand, is a structured research method used to measure and quantify data using numerical methods. Quantitative research involves collecting and analysing data through surveys, experiments, and statistical analysis. The goal of quantitative research is to measure and quantify consumer behaviours, attitudes, and opinions in a way that can be analysed statistically. Quantitative research is beneficial when researchers have a specific hypothesis to test or when they need to make accurate predictions about consumer behaviours.

For example, a market researcher conducting a quantitative research project on consumer preferences for a new food product may survey a large sample of consumers using a structured questionnaire. The questionnaire may include closed-ended questions with pre-defined response options that can be analysed quantitatively. The researcher may then use statistical analysis to identify relationships between variables, such as demographic characteristics and product preferences.

How Small Businesses Can Conduct Marketing Research

Small businesses may not have the resources to conduct extensive marketing research, but there are several methods they can use to gather information about their customers and competitors.

Online Surveys: Online surveys can be a cost-effective way for small businesses to gather customer information. Several online survey tools are available that are easy to use and provide valuable data.

Social Media: Social media platforms such as Facebook and Twitter can be used to gather information about customers and competitors. Small businesses can monitor social media conversations to identify trends and customer needs.

Customer Feedback: Small businesses can gather customer feedback through in-person interactions, email, or online surveys. This feedback can provide valuable insights into customer needs and preferences.

Competitive Analysis: Small businesses can conduct a competitive analysis by researching competitors' websites, social media profiles, and marketing materials. This can help them identify competitive advantages and weaknesses.

Designing a Marketing Research Survey

Designing a marketing survey for a new product launch is essential in ensuring its success in the market. The survey should provide valuable insights into customer preferences and help the business identify critical areas for improvement. Here are some steps to follow when designing a marketing survey for a new product launch:

1. **Define the research objectives:** For example, is the business looking to identify the target audience, determine the pricing strategy, or measure customer satisfaction? Having clear research objectives will help design relevant and actionable questions.

2. **Determine the survey methodology:** Will it be an online survey, a phone survey, or a face-to-face interview? Choose the method that will give the best response rate and data quality.

3. **Develop the survey questions:** Start with general questions and then move to more specific ones. Consider using open-ended questions to allow customers to share their opinions and ideas in their own words. Also, avoid leading or biased questions that may influence the responses.

4. **Test the survey:** Test the survey on a small group of people to identify any problems with the questions, flow, or length of the survey. Revise and refine the survey as necessary.

5. **Distribute the survey:** Once finalised, distribute it to the target audience. Make sure to include a clear introduction

and explain the purpose of the survey. Offer an incentive, such as a discount or prize, to encourage participation.

6. **Analyse the results:** After collecting the responses, analyse the data to identify patterns and trends. Use the findings to inform the marketing strategy, product development, and customer engagement.

Research helps businesses make informed decisions about its marketing strategies.

See also:

Market Analysis: Insights
Market Analysis: Bias in Research
Marketing Measurement: Data Analysis

Chapter 13

Bias in Research

Research is an essential aspect of making informed business decisions. However, it is necessary to understand that research is only partially objective, as various biases can affect the results. Biases can influence how research is conducted, analysed, and interpreted, while leading to inaccurate or misleading conclusions. This chapter will provide an overview of possible biases to watch out for, including Champion Bias, Herding, Anchoring, Confirmation, Loss Aversion, and Overoptimism.

Champion Bias is the tendency of researchers to overemphasise positive feedback or results that support their hypothesis or beliefs. This bias can lead to selective interpretation or omission of data, leading to a skewed or inaccurate view of the research results. For example, say a researcher is invested in the success of a new product launch. In that case, they may focus only on the positive feedback from early adopters, ignoring negative feedback or critiques that could help improve the product.

Herding bias is the tendency to follow trends or popular opinions in research rather than analyse the data objectively. This bias can be influenced by the need to conform to social norms and expectations, or the desire to be perceived as part of a successful group. For example, suppose a researcher sees that a particular research method or technique is trendy. In that case, they may choose to use it, even if it is not the most appropriate or effective method for their research question.

Anchoring bias is the tendency for researchers to rely too heavily on the initial information presented to them when making decisions or concluding. This bias can influence the interpretation of research data, as researchers may be more likely to focus on information that confirms their initial beliefs or hypotheses rather than exploring alternative explanations. For example, suppose a researcher believes their new product will succeed in a particular market. In that case, they may anchor their research analysis around data that supports this belief, rather than exploring alternative explanations or considering the potential limitations of their product.

Confirmation bias is the tendency for researchers to seek out and interpret information that supports their pre-existing beliefs or hypotheses. This bias can be problematic as it can lead to researchers ignoring or dismissing data that contradicts their beliefs, resulting in a skewed or inaccurate interpretation of research results. For example, suppose a researcher believes their new marketing campaign will succeed. In that case, they may selectively seek and interpret data supporting this belief while ignoring data suggesting otherwise.

Loss aversion bias is the tendency for researchers to overemphasise the potential losses associated with their research findings rather than focusing on potential gains. This bias can lead to researchers needing to be more cautious or risk-averse, potentially missing out on opportunities for growth or innovation. For example, suppose a researcher finds that their new product launch may have some associated limitations or risks. In that case, they may overemphasise these potential losses and be hesitant to move forward with the launch rather than consider potential gains and opportunities for growth.

Overoptimism bias is the tendency for researchers to be overly optimistic about their research findings or outcomes, leading to unrealistic or overly optimistic conclusions. This bias can be influenced by a desire to be perceived as successful or by a lack of critical evaluation of research data. For example, suppose a researcher finds that their new marketing campaign has received positive feedback. In that case, they may overemphasise this feedback and draw overly optimistic conclusions about the campaign's success without considering potential limitations or areas for improvement.

Overall, it is essential to be aware of possible biases in research and take steps to minimise their impact. All data collected should be accurate, representative, and reliable. Here are some ways to minimise the impact of bias in marketing research:

Step 1 Clearly define the research question: Before conducting any research, it's important to define the research question clearly. This helps to ensure that the research is focused and relevant, and that the data collected is meaningful.

Step 2 Use multiple data collection methods: Using multiple data collection methods, such as surveys, interviews, and focus groups, can help to reduce bias in marketing research. Each method provides a different perspective on the research question and helps to ensure that the data collected is comprehensive and unbiased.

Step 3 Randomize sampling: Random sampling is a technique that involves selecting participants randomly from a population. This helps to ensure that the sample is representative of the population and that there is no bias in the selection process.

Step 4 Avoid leading questions: Leading questions are questions that are designed to elicit a particular response from participants. They can introduce bias into the research by influencing the reactions of participants. Avoiding leading questions. Using neutral language in surveys and interviews is important.

Step 5 Conduct pilot testing: Pilot testing involves testing the research instrument, such as a survey or interview guide, on a small sample of participants before conducting the full study. This helps to identify and address any issues with the research instrument before the complete study is conducted, which can help to reduce bias.

Step 6 Analyse data objectively: It's important to analyse the data objectively, without preconceived notions or biases. This involves using appropriate statistical methods to analyse the data, draw conclusions, and be open to unexpected findings.

Step 7 Use diverse research teams: Using diverse research teams can help to minimise bias in marketing research. This is because a diverse team can bring different perspectives and experiences to the research, which can help to ensure that the research is comprehensive and unbiased.

Marketing Research Gone Wrong

In the mid-1950s, Ford Motor Company set out to create a new line of cars that would revolutionise the industry. The company invested heavily in market research, hoping to develop a vehicle appealing to American consumers' changing tastes and preferences. The result was the Ford Edsel, which would become one of the biggest flops in automotive history.

Ford's marketing research before launching the Edsel was extensive but ultimately flawed. The company relied heavily on consumer surveys and focus groups, which provided a skewed perspective on what customers wanted. In addition, Ford's research failed to account for changing economic conditions and shifting consumer trends.

The Edsel was introduced to the public in 1957 with much fanfare and anticipation. However, it quickly became clear that the car was a disappointment. The car's odd styling and gimmicky features put consumers off, such as the push-button transmission and the 'horse-collar' grille. In addition, the Edsel was priced too high for its target market, which was already feeling the effects of an economic downturn.

Despite Ford's best efforts to salvage the brand, the Edsel was discontinued just three years after its launch. The failure of the Edsel cost Ford millions of dollars in lost revenue and damaged the company's reputation. Ultimately, it was a case of a company relying too heavily on market research and failing to accurately gauge consumer preferences and economic conditions.

Companies must take a holistic approach to understand their customers and the market and be prepared to adapt to changing conditions. Simply relying on consumer surveys and focus groups is insufficient to guarantee success in today's competitive business environment.

Be aware that bias is inevitable in research and create appropriate methods to analyse the data before making business decisions.

See also:

Market Analysis: Insights
Market Analysis: Marketing Research

III
Brand Building

Chapter 15

Marketing & Branding

Marketing and branding are two terms that are often used interchangeably in the business world. However, they are distinct concepts that serve different purposes. This chapter will explore the difference between marketing and branding and their respective roles in building a successful business.

Marketing

Marketing is about creating, communicating, delivering, and exchanging value offerings for customers, clients, partners, and society. Activities include market research, product development, pricing, advertising, sales promotions, and customer service. The aim is to create customer awareness and interest in a company's products or services, and persuade customers to purchase.

In addition, it's a broad term that encompasses many different activities and channels. These include traditional advertising, such as television, radio, and print ads, and digital marketing channels, such as social media, email marketing, and search engine optimisation (SEO).

Marketing is critical to the success of any business because it helps identify and target ideal customers, understand needs and preferences, and develop products and services that meet those needs. It also allows firms to differentiate themselves from competitors and build a strong brand identity.

Branding

Branding, on the other hand, is the process of creating a unique name, image, or symbol that identifies and differentiates a product or service from those of other companies. By creating a unique personality, voice, and message, marketers hope to create a product that resonates with customers and communicates the company's values and mission.

A strong brand can help businesses to build customer loyalty, increase brand recognition, and improve their reputation. Brands can also command a premium price, increasing profitability and market share.

The Difference between Marketing and Branding

While marketing functions as the overarching umbrella, branding is only one spoke. So while marketing and branding are closely related, there are some key differences between the two concepts.

Focus
Marketing is focused on the tactical aspects of promoting a product or service, such as identifying the target audience, developing messaging, and creating advertising campaigns. Branding, on the other hand, is focused on the strategic aspects of creating a brand identity that aligns with the company's mission, values, and vision.

Purpose
The purpose of marketing is to drive sales and revenue by promoting products or services to customers. On the other hand, branding aims to build a strong brand identity that resonates with customers and creates a loyal following.

Scope

Marketing encompasses various activities and channels, including advertising, sales promotions, and customer service. On the other hand, branding is focused on creating a unique brand identity that encompasses all aspects of the company's operations, including customer service, product development, and employee culture.

Outcome

The marketing outcome is typically measured in terms of sales, revenue, and ROI. On the other hand, the outcome of branding is measured in terms of brand recognition, customer loyalty, and reputation.

A great example to illustrate this is Coca-Cola. The company has been successful in building a strong brand identity over the years. The company's iconic logo, trademarked colours, and signature bottle shape are instantly recognisable to consumers worldwide. Coca-Cola's overall marketing focuses on reinforcing the brand markers and creating an emotional connection with consumers. The company's advertisements often feature happy people sharing a Coca-Cola, emphasising the idea of a universal bond that the product creates.

Marketing and branding are distinct concepts that serve different purposes.

See also:

Market Fundamentals: What is Marketing?
Brand Building: Brand Positioning
Marketing Communication: Marketing & Advertising

Chapter 16

Brand Positioning

Brand positioning is a critical aspect of marketing strategy. It involves creating a distinctive image and value proposition for a brand from the consumers' perspective. Effective brand positioning sets a brand apart from its competitors, communicates the unique benefits of the brand, and builds strong emotional connections with target customers. This chapter will provide an overview of brand positioning, its components, and how it can be done effectively.

What is Brand Positioning?

It is the art of identifying and communicating the key differentiators that set a brand apart from its competitors. Not only is brand positioning about what a company does and sells, but brand positioning is also about how it communicates with its customers and what values it represents.

Some of the world's favourite brands have effectively positioned themselves in the markets. Some examples of effective brand positioning include:

Zara: Zara is a Spanish fashion brand known for its trendy and affordable clothing. The company's products are designed to be on-trend and fashion-forward, with new collections released frequently to keep up with the latest styles.

IKEA: IKEA is a Swedish furniture and home goods brand known for its affordable and functional designs. The company's products are designed to be simple and easy to assemble, with a focus on clean lines and minimalist aesthetics.

Glossier: Glossier's brand positioning is predicated on the idea of 'skincare and makeup for real life'. The company's products are designed to be natural, easy to use, and suitable to wear on a daily basis. Glossier's brand messaging is designed to appeal to young and busy women who want to look good without spending a lot of time or money on their beauty routines.

But size is not always a guarantor of success. Even big brands sometimes get it wrong, as the following examples show:

JCPenney: In 2012, JCPenney rebranded itself as a store without sales and discounts, hoping to attract a new customer base. However, this strategy was a disaster, and sales plummeted as customers were no longer motivated to shop at the store without the allure of discounts. This shows that JCPenney failed to understand its customers' motivations and the importance of sales promotions in the retail industry.

BlackBerry: Once a dominant player in the smartphone market, BlackBerry failed to adapt to the rise of touchscreen devices and the popularity of app stores. As a result, the company lost its market share to competitors such as Apple and Samsung. This shows that BlackBerry failed to fathom the evolving needs and preferences and the importance of innovation in the technology industry.

Kodak: Kodak was a market leader in the photography industry for over a century but failed to adapt to the rise of digital photography. The company held on to its traditional film-based business model for too long, and by the time it tried to pivot to digital, it was too late. This shows that Kodak failed to understand the changing technology landscape and its customers' evolving needs and preferences.

Positioning a business's brand is probably one of the most first tasks in marketing. So it's therefore important to understand that this is not a one-step process but includes multiple key components that build on each other:

Target Audience: Defining the target audience is a necessary component of brand positioning. It involves identifying the target market's demographics, psychographics, and behaviours. Understanding the target audience helps to create messages that resonate with them and build strong emotional connections.

Unique Value Proposition: A brand's unique value proposition (UVP) is the core benefit or promise that sets it apart from competitors. It is a statement communicating what makes the brand unique and valuable to the target audience. The UVP should be compelling, memorable, and resonate with the target market's needs and desires.

Brand Personality: Brand personality is the set of human characteristics associated with a brand. It is the emotional connection that the brand creates with its customers. The brand personality should align with the values and aspirations of the target market and should be consistently communicated through all marketing channels.

Brand Positioning Statement: The brand positioning statement concisely summarises the key components of brand positioning. It should include the target audience, the unique value proposition, and the brand personality. The brand positioning statement should be easily understood and communicated to all stakeholders.

Unique Value Proposition

Coming up with a UVP can be daunting, but it's imperative to identify for businesses why consumers would choose their product over anyone else's. However minor the difference between the product or service is, as long as it hits a pain point, it becomes relevant at the point of purchase.

There are multiple possible unique selling points and key differentiators that a product or service can have. Here are some examples:

Innovative features or technology: If the product or service has unique and innovative features or uses cutting-edge technology, this can be a strong selling point.

Superior quality or performance: If the product or service is known for its high quality, superior performance, or exceptional durability, this can accentuate the business. **Competitive pricing:** Offering a lower price point than competitors can be a fundamental differentiator, especially if the company can maintain high quality and performance.

Exceptional customer service: Providing exceptional customer service can be a unique selling point, as customers are often willing to pay more for a better experience.

Personalisation: If the product or service offers a high level of personalisation or customisation, this can be a strong selling point.

Environmental sustainability: If the product or service is environmentally friendly, this can appeal to consumers concerned about sustainability.

Convenience: If the product or service offers convenience such as fast delivery or easy accessibility this can be advantageous.

Reputation and trust: If the brand has a strong reputation for quality, reliability, or trustworthiness, this can be a differentiator.

Unique selling points and differentiators will vary depending on the product or service, industry, and target market. Companies should research the market and competitors to identify what sets the company apart and how it can leverage this to attract customers.

Brand Personality - The 12 Archetypes

The concept of brand archetypes was first introduced by Swiss psychologist Carl Jung, who believed that archetypes were universal patterns of behaviour and personality that exist within the collective unconscious of all humans. Jung's work on archetypes inspired marketing experts Margaret Mark and Carol Pearson to develop the concept of brand archetypes in the late 1990s, arguing that they could be used to create more powerful and effective branding strategies.

Brand archetypes are useful to businesses because they provide a framework for creating a brand personality that resonates with customers on a deeper level. By identifying and embodying a particular archetype, businesses can establish a more meaningful and emotional connection with their target audience by identifying and embodying a particular archetype. This can help to differentiate a brand from its competitors and create a more loyal customer base.

Additionally, brand archetypes provide a way to maintain a consistent brand identity across all marketing channels and touchpoints. By using the same archetype to guide all messaging and visual branding elements, businesses can create a cohesive and recognisable brand identity instantly recognisable to customers.

- **The Innocent:** Pure, optimistic, and simple. Examples include Coca-Cola, Innocent Smoothies, and Dove.

- **The Explorer:** Adventurous, independent, and curious. Examples include The North Face, Patagonia, and Jeep.

- **The Sage:** Knowledgeable, wise, and rational. Examples include Harvard University, The New York Times, and TED Talks.

- **The Hero:** Brave, determined, and courageous. Examples include Nike, Apple, and Superman.

- **The Outlaw:** Rebellious, provocative, and daring. Examples include Harley Davidson, Diesel, and Red Bull.

- **The Magician:** Creative, imaginative, and transformative. Examples include Disney, Apple, and Tesla.

- **The Regular Guy/Girl:** Relatable, friendly, and trustworthy. Examples include Ikea, McDonald's, and Gap.

- **The Lover:** Sensual, passionate, and intimate. Examples include Victoria's Secret, Chanel, and Godiva.

- **The Jester:** Humorous, entertaining, and playful. Examples include M&M's, Old Spice, and Geico.

- **The Caregiver:** Nurturing, compassionate, and supportive. Examples include Johnson & Johnson, UNICEF, and Toms.

- **The Creator:** Artistic, innovative, and visionary. Examples include Lego, Apple, and Adobe.

- **The Ruler:** Authoritative, powerful, and dominant. Examples include Rolex, Mercedes-Benz, and American Express.

Some brands may embody a mix of archetypes or evolve to embody a different archetype as their brand identity changes. Additionally, the same archetype can be used by different brands in different ways, depending on their target audience, industry, and values.

Understanding the brand's archetype can help create more effective and targeted messaging and establish a more coherent and consistent brand identity.

Brand Positioning Statement

Last but not least, building on the previous steps, the positioning statement should communicate the brand's unique value proposition and differentiate it from competitors. It should be concise, memorable, and easy to understand. A good positioning statement typically includes the following components:

- **Target market:** Identifies the specific group of customers that the brand is targeting.

- **Unique selling proposition:** Describes the brand's unique offering or benefit that sets it apart from competitors.

- **Benefit:** Explain the specific benefit the target customer will receive from the brand.

- **Reason to believe:** Provides evidence or proof that the brand can deliver its promise.

Here's an example of a well-crafted positioning statement:

'For busy and health-conscious professionals who want to eat nutritiously on the go, our meal delivery service offers delicious and chef-prepared meals made from locally sourced and organic ingredients which are conveniently delivered to your door. Our unique blend of convenience and quality ensures you'll never have to sacrifice healthy eating for a busy schedule'.

On the other hand, a poorly crafted positioning statement can lead to confusion, lack of differentiation, and, ultimately, failure. For example:

'We offer a range of high-quality, affordable products that are perfect for anyone looking for something good'.

This positioning statement is vague and does not provide any specific information about what the brand offers or who it targets. It fails to differentiate the brand from competitors and gives no reason to believe that the products are high quality.

Common Mistakes in Brand Positioning

Overall, brand positioning is pivotal to a successful marketing strategy. But often, it takes multiple tries and time to get it right, so it's essential to watch out for the most common mistakes.

If the brand positioning is too broad and generic, it might not stand out in the marketplace. For example, if a clothing brand positions itself as selling 'affordable and trendy clothes for everyone', it does not give customers any specific reason to choose them over similar brands.

While it's important to highlight the features and benefits of the products or services, solely focusing on these aspects can lead to ineffective brand positioning. For example, a phone manufacturer might position itself as having the best camera quality. Still, if that's the only selling point, it might not be enough to differentiate the brand from competitors.

Effective brand positioning is all about meeting the needs and desires of the target customers. Ignoring these needs can lead to ineffective positioning. For example, a luxury car brand that positions itself as the most affordable option might not resonate with customers looking for a high-end and luxury experience.

Consistency is key when it comes to effective brand positioning. If a brand's messaging and positioning change frequently, it can confuse customers and complicate building a solid brand identity. For example, if a coffee shop positions itself as a cosy and family-friendly environment one week and a hipster hangout the next, it might struggle to attract and retain customers.

While it's essential to stay aware of competitor positioning and messaging, copying them can lead to ineffective brand positioning. Customers will see the brand as a copycat and may not see a reason to switch from the original brand. For example, if a fast food restaurant positions itself as offering the same menu as a popular competitor but at a slightly lower price, it might not be enough to convince customers to switch.

Brand positioning is how a brand shows up to consumers.

See also:

Market Analysis: Consumer Profiling
Market Analysis: Competition
Market Analysis: Bowman's Strategic Clock
Market Analysis: The Blue Ocean Strategy
Marketing Mix: Product
Marketing Mix: Price
Marketing Mix: Promotion
Marketing Mix: Place

IV
Marketing Mix

Chapter 17

The 6 P Framework

The 6P concept in marketing is a framework that helps businesses develop a comprehensive and effective marketing strategy. The 6Ps consists of Product, Price, Promotion, Place, People, and Process. Each element is important in the marketing mix and can significantly impact a company's success.

The product is a company's core offering and is what customers ultimately pay for. To be successful, businesses must ensure that their products meet the needs and wants of their target audience. This involves developing high-quality and reliable products that offer unique benefits or features.

Pricing is another key element of the marketing mix. Businesses must set competitive prices and reflect the value of their products or services. This involves understanding the production costs, analysing competitors' prices, and considering the product's perceived value in the consumer's eyes.

Promotion refers to the various marketing tactics a company uses to communicate with their target audience and persuade them to purchase. This can include advertising, public relations, direct marketing, and sales promotions.

Place refers to the distribution channels that a company uses to get their products or services into the hands of the consumer. This can involve selecting suitable retail locations, setting up an online store, or partnering with distributors or wholesalers.

People refers to the people who buy the product and the employees who represent the company and interact with customers. Businesses must ensure their employees are knowledgeable, friendly, and can provide excellent customer service.

Process refers to the procedures and systems that a company uses to deliver their products or services to customers. This can include everything from the ordering process, to the delivery of the product or service.

By considering each of these 6Ps, businesses can develop a comprehensive and effective marketing strategy tailored to their target audience's needs and wants. Whether a company is launching a new product, entering a new market, or trying to increase sales, the 6Ps concept can provide a framework for success regardless of size.

The 6P Marketing Mix concept is a tool to understand what aspects of a business are impacted by marketing and its resulting consumer insights. Here's an example of how the 6P marketing mix might be applied to a small business that sells handmade candles:

Product: The business offers a variety of high-quality and all-natural candles in various scents and sizes. The candles are made with eco-friendly ingredients, and are packaged in attractive and reusable containers.

Price: The business has analysed production costs and competitors' prices to set a fair price for their candles. They offer various price points to appeal to different types of customers, with smaller candles priced lower, and larger candles priced higher.

Promotion: The business uses a combination of social media advertising, influencer marketing, and email marketing to promote its candles. They create eye-catching graphics and photographs to showcase their products and run regular promotions and sales to entice customers to purchase.

Place: The business sells its candles through its website and a few local retail locations. They also offer free shipping to customers who order a certain amount of candles online.

People: At the core of marketing is the relationship between customers and the product. While most businesses focus on the product, a strong empahsis should also be placed on customer service and ensuring that employees know about their products and can answer customer questions. They also use customer feedback to improve their products and services continuously.

Process: The business has a smooth ordering and fulfilment process to ensure customers receive their candles promptly and efficiently. They carefully package each candle to ensure it arrives in perfect condition and offer easy returns and exchanges for any issues.

By carefully considering each of these 6Ps, the business in this example can develop a comprehensive and effective marketing strategy that helps them stand out in a crowded market and attract loyal customers who appreciate its high-quality and eco-friendly candles.

Limitations of the 6P model

Whilst this framework provides a comprehensive approach to marketing management, it has some limitations that need to be considered.

Complexity: The addition of three new elements (people, process, and physical evidence) to the traditional 4P framework can make it more complex to use and understand. This complexity can make it difficult for businesses to apply the framework practically.

Limited applicability: The 6P framework is most applicable to service businesses where the physical evidence, people, and process play a significant role in the customer's experience. For product-based businesses, these elements may have limited applicability, and the traditional 4P framework may be more appropriate.

Lack of prioritisation: The framework does not provide clear guidance on how to prioritise the different elements. This can lead to a lack of focus, and to spreading resources too thin across all six elements, rather than prioritising the most important ones.

Limited emphasis on customer needs: The framework can be internally focused, emphasising the business's capabilities and processes rather than the needs of the customer. This can result in a mismatch between the business's offerings and the customer's needs.

Cultural differences: The people element of the 6P framework may translate poorly across different cultures. Different cultures may have different expectations of service and interaction with people, making it challenging to apply the framework universally.

In the following six chapters, we will go through each component of this concept in detail with examples.

The 6Ps are the building block of any marketing strategy.

See also:

Marketing Mix: Product
Marketing Mix: Price
Marketing Mix: Promotion
Marketing Mix: Place
Marketing Mix: People
Marketing Mix: Process

Product

The product element of the marketing mix is a central component of any successful marketing strategy. The product is what a company offers to customers, and it can take a number of forms, including physical goods, services, and even ideas. In this section, we will discuss the importance of the product element of the marketing mix and its crucial role in marketing strategy.

Product development is the process of creating new products or improving existing ones. This is the starting point for all other marketing activities. A company must create products that meet the needs and wants of its target market. This requires a deep understanding of customer needs, preferences, and behaviour.

Once a company has developed a product, it must determine the appropriate pricing, distribution, and promotional strategies to market the product effectively. This will be covered in the following chapters on the remaining Ps that form the Marketing Mix.

The product element of the marketing mix includes four key components: product design, branding, packaging, and labelling.

Product Design

Product design is the process of creating a product that meets the needs and wants of customers. This includes determining the product's features, benefits, and overall design. A well-designed product can set a company apart and create a strong brand identity.

Branding

Branding creates a unique name, design, and image for a product or service. A strong brand can create a loyal customer base and increase brand recognition. A company's branding strategy should reflect the values, personality, and image they want to project to its target market.

Packaging

Packaging is the physical container that holds the product. It serves many functions, including protecting the product during transportation and storage, providing meaningful product information to customers, and creating a distinctive look and feel. Adequate packaging can influence a customer's purchasing decision and increase brand recognition.

Labelling

Labelling provides important information about the product, including ingredients, nutritional information, and usage instructions. This is required by law and is important for ensuring customers make informed decisions. In addition, labelling can also be used as a marketing tool to differentiate a product from its competitors.

The product element sets the foundation for all other marketing activities. A well-designed and branded product can create a solid emotional connection with customers, leading to increased brand loyalty and repeat purchases. In addition, a product that meets the needs and wants of its target market can generate positive word-of-mouth advertising which is a powerful marketing tool.

Product development also plays a crucial role in the product life cycle. As a product moves through its life cycle, it may require updates or modifications to remain relevant and meet the changing needs of its target market. Effective product development can help a company stay ahead of its competitors and maintain market share.

How to Develop a Product

Developing a new product for a business can be complex, but following a step-by-step guide can help companies to stay organised and focused on their goals. Here is a general guide to developing a product for the business:

Identify the Need

The first step in developing a new product is identifying a need in the market that is not currently being met. This may involve researching trends, talking to potential customers, and analysing data.

Define the Product

Once a need has been identified, the company must define the product to create. This involves deciding on the product features, design, and functionality.

Conduct Market Research

Market research is essential for understanding the target market and determining the potential demand for the product. This can involve surveys, focus groups, and analysing data on customer behaviour and preferences.

Develop a Prototype

A prototype is a preliminary product model that can be tested and refined. This can involve creating sketches, 3D models, or functional prototypes.

Test and Refine

Testing the prototype with potential customers and getting feedback is essential for identifying areas for improvement and making adjustments to the design or functionality of the product.

Finalise Design

Once the product has been refined based on customer feedback, it's time to finalise the design. This may involve creating detailed technical drawings, selecting materials, and determining the manufacturing process.

Develop a Marketing Plan

A marketing plan is essential for promoting the product and generating sales. This involves identifying the target market, determining the pricing strategy, and developing promotional materials and advertising campaigns.

Launch the Product

Launching the product involves bringing it to market and making it available to customers. This may involve setting up distribution channels, creating packaging, and organising a launch event.

Evaluate Performance

After launching the product, the next step is to evaluate its performance and make adjustments as necessary. This may involve analysing sales data, monitoring customer feedback, and changing the marketing strategy.

The Importance of Packaging

Packaging is often the first point of contact between a customer and a product. It can attract attention, communicate information about the product, and influence purchasing decisions. Packaging can be critical in differentiating a product from its competitors in today's crowded marketplace. A well-designed package can help a product stand out on the shelves and make a lasting impression on potential customers.

Packaging also plays a vital role in brand recognition and brand image. A distinctive package design can help establish a brand identity and communicate the brand's values and personality. For example, Coca-Cola's iconic bottle design has symbolised its heritage and values, contributing to its worldwide recognition.

Moments of Truth

A useful concept to evaluate packaging and its impact on the consumer journey is Procter & Gamble's Moments of Truth (MOT). It refers to the critical points in a consumer's interaction with a brand or product and was first introduced by former P&G CEO A.G. Lafley in 2005 and has since become a widely recognised framework in the marketing industry. The MOT concept is based on the idea that there are three critical moments in a consumer's decision-making process:

The First Moment of Truth occurs when a consumer is standing in front of a product on the shelf, deciding whether to purchase it or not. The packaging, design, and overall presentation of the product play a crucial role in this moment.

The Second Moment of Truth occurs when a consumer uses the product for the first time and forms an opinion about its quality and effectiveness. The product's performance and the overall user experience are pivotal at this moment.

The Third Moment of Truth occurs when a consumer shares their experience with others through word-of-mouth or online reviews. Positive feedback can lead to increased brand loyalty, while negative feedback can significantly impact a brand's reputation.

The MOT concept accentuates the importance of understanding the consumer's perspective and designing products and marketing strategies that cater to their needs and preferences. By focusing on these key moments, companies can identify areas for improvement and develop targeted marketing campaigns to enhance the consumer experience.

P&G has also developed a Fourth Moment of Truth, which refers to the ongoing relationship between the consumer and the brand. This involves building brand loyalty and fostering long-term customer relationships through ongoing engagement and communication.

Overall, the Moments of Truth concept has become an essential framework for marketers to understand and improve the consumer experience. By focusing on these critical moments, companies can gain valuable insights into consumer behaviour and develop effective marketing strategies to drive growth and build brand loyalty.

Effective Packaging Components

To create effective packaging, there are several components that companies should consider:

Functionality: The primary function of packaging is to protect the product during transportation and storage. The package must withstand the rigours of the distribution process while also being easy for the customer to open and use.

Information: Packaging should provide essential information about the product, such as its ingredients, nutritional information, and usage instructions. This can help customers make informed purchasing decisions and ensure that they use the product correctly.

Branding: Packaging should reflect the brand's values and personality while being visually appealing and eye-catching. The package design should be distinctive and memorable and communicate with the brand's unique identity.

Sustainability: As consumers become more environmentally conscious, sustainability has become an increasingly decisive factor in packaging design. Companies should consider using eco-friendly materials and reducing waste in their packaging.

Examples of Successful Product Packaging

Apple's iPhone Packaging: Apple's iPhone packaging is a prime example of effective packaging design. The sleek and minimalist design reflects the brand's commitment to simplicity and innovation. The packaging includes only essential information, and the product is easy to remove and use.

McDonald's French Fries Container: McDonald's iconic French Fries container has become a recognisable symbol of the brand. The container's unique shape and bold colours make it stand out and reinforce the brand's playful personality.

Dove's Body Wash Packaging: Dove's body wash packaging is designed to appeal to women of all shapes and sizes. The packaging features a range of body types, reflecting the brand's commitment to promoting positive body image. The package design is also eco-friendly, using 100% recycled plastic.

A company must create products that meet the needs and wants of its target market.

See also:

Market Analysis: Marketing Research
Market Analysis: Bias in Research
Market Analysis: Insights

Chapter 19

Price

Pricing is a critical element of the marketing mix, and it's essential to a company's overall marketing strategy. The price of a product or service can affect a company's revenue, profitability, and market share and impact customer perceptions and purchase behaviour. In this chapter, we will explore the importance of pricing in marketing strategy and provide an overview of the most common pricing strategies.

The Role of Pricing

Pricing is critical to a company's marketing strategy because it directly impacts revenue, profitability, and market share. The price of a product or service can influence customer perceptions of values, qualities, and prestige and also affect customer purchase behaviour. A company's pricing strategy can determine whether it is perceived as a value-oriented or luxury brand. It can also impact its ability to compete with other companies in the market.

Pricing is also closely linked to a company's overall business strategy. For example, suppose a company is focused on maximising revenue and profitability. In that case, it may adopt a premium pricing strategy, while a company focused on market share may adopt a low-cost pricing strategy. The pricing strategy should align with the company's overall business strategy and objectives to be effective.

Price Elasticity

Before going into the most common price strategies, it's worth understanding the concept of Price elasticity. The term refers to the responsiveness of demand or quantity demanded to changes in the price of a product or service. It measures the degree to which consumers' purchasing behaviour is influenced by price fluctuations. Price elasticity is a fundamental economic concept and plays a crucial role in understanding the dynamics between value and volume.

The elasticity coefficient is used to quantify the responsiveness of demand. It is calculated as the percentage change in quantity demanded divided by the percentage change in price. The resulting value can be positive, negative, or zero. A positive value indicates elastic demand, meaning that a change in price leads to a relatively larger change in quantity demanded. A negative value indicates inelastic demand, where the quantity demanded changes by a smaller proportion than the price. A coefficient of zero represents perfectly inelastic demand, where the quantity demanded remains constant regardless of price changes.

When demand is elastic, a price change substantially affects the quantity demanded. If a business lowers the price of a product with elastic demand, consumers respond by purchasing more of it, increasing in volume. Conversely, if the price is raised, consumers may reduce their purchases, decreasing volume. Therefore, the relationship between value (price) and volume is inversely proportional when dealing with elastic demand.

On the other hand, when demand is inelastic, price changes have a relatively smaller effect on the quantity demanded. In this case, a price decrease may not lead to a substantial increase in volume, as consumers' demand is less sensitive to price fluctuations. Similarly, a price increase may not result in a significant decrease in volume. The relationship between value and volume in the context of inelastic demand is less pronounced and exhibits a weaker inverse proportionality compared to elastic demand.

The degree of price elasticity can vary across different products, industries, and market segments. Certain goods, such as luxury or non-essential goods, often exhibit more elastic demand. This is because consumers have more flexibility in purchasing decisions for these products. Conversely, essential goods like food or medications tend to have inelastic demand since consumers are less likely to alter their consumption patterns drastically based on price changes.

Based on Ehrenberg-Bass Research's analysis of dozens of categories and products, the average price elasticity is -2.5%. That means if the price goes up by 1%, sales are expected to go down by 2.5%. It is important to note that price elasticity is not the sole determinant of consumer behaviour. Other factors, such as consumer preferences, income levels, availability of substitutes, and market competition, also influence demand. Additionally, price elasticity can change over time as consumer preferences and market conditions evolve.

Common Pricing Strategies

There are many different pricing strategies that companies can use to achieve their marketing and business objectives. Some of the most common pricing strategies include:

- **Cost-Plus Pricing:** Cost-plus pricing involves adding a markup to the cost of the product or service to determine the final price. Companies often use this approach focused on maximising profitability, ensuring that the company covers its costs and generates a profit on each sale.

- **Value-Based Pricing:** Value-based pricing involves setting the price based on the perceived value of the product or service to the customer. This approach is often used by companies focused on creating a premium brand image and attracting customers willing to pay more for higher quality or prestige.

- **Penetration Pricing:** Penetration pricing involves setting a low price initially to attract customers and gain market share. New entrants often use this approach to a market or by companies that are looking to increase their market share quickly.

- **Skimming Pricing:** Skimming pricing involves setting a high price initially to take advantage of customer demand for a new or innovative product. This approach is often used by companies focused on maximising revenue and profitability in the short term.

- **Dynamic Pricing:** Dynamic pricing involves changing prices based on market conditions, such as supply and demand, time of day, or customer behaviours. This approach is often used by companies focused on maximising revenue and profitability by optimising prices in real-time. Nowadays, Dynamic pricing is a sophisticated and fully automated process used by, for example, gas stations, train companies and airlines.

- **Bundling Pricing:** Bundling pricing involves offering multiple products or services at a discounted price. Companies often use this approach to increase sales of multiple products or services simultaneously or to introduce a new product by piggybacking off an already successful product. A specific example would be perfume companies selling bundles of perfumes and matching shower gels to drive the trial of the secondary product and drive the overall value perception of the purchase.

- **Psychological Pricing:** This relies on understanding consumer behaviours and behavioural psychology to set prices that trigger specific responses. One common approach is to use odd pricing, which involves setting prices just below round numbers (e.g. $9.99 instead of $10.00). This creates the perception of a lower price and encourages more purchases.

- **Price Anchoring**: A high-priced item is placed next to a lower-priced item to make it seem like a better value. For example, a watch worth $1,000 placed next to a $500 watch worth $500 can make the $500 watch seem like a good deal. This is often used for online services when gold, silver, or bronze tiering is offered. Customers are more likely to choose the 'golden middle' when given the choice.

Examples of Pricing Strategies in Action

To better understand how pricing strategies can be used in marketing and business strategy, let's look at real-world examples.

Apple's Value-Based Pricing: Apple is known for its premium pricing strategy, which is based on the perceived value of its products to customers. For example, an iPhone is priced higher than many other smartphones in the market, but it is still popular because customers believe it offers higher quality and better features.

Walmart's Low-Cost Pricing: Walmart is known for its low-cost pricing strategy, which is based on offering products at a lower price than its competitors. This approach has allowed Walmart to gain market share and become a dominant player in the retail industry.

Amazon's Dynamic Pricing: Amazon uses dynamic pricing to optimise its prices in real time based on market conditions.

Types of Promotional Pricing

Promotional pricing, in particular, is a well-used method to drive sales and is closely related to the next P in the marketing mix, promotion. The goal is to increase demand and attract customers by reducing the price of a product or service. Promotional pricing can also differentiate a product from competitors and attract new customers. However, businesses should be careful not to overuse promotional pricing, which can create a perception of low quality or erode profit margins. Here are some of the different types of promotional pricing and when businesses should use them:

- **Loss Leaders:** A loss leader is a product that is sold at a loss to attract customers who will hopefully purchase other profitable products as well. Grocery stores often use this strategy, where they might sell certain items, such as milk or bread, at a very low price to get people in the door and then lead them to spend on other higher-value items impulsively.

- **Bundling:** Bundling is when a business sells multiple products or services at a discounted price. This strategy can be effective for businesses with various related products, such as software companies or telecommunications-providers. For example, a telecommunication provider might offer a bundle package that includes cable TV, internet, and phone services at a discounted price.

- **Coupons:** Coupons are a common form of promotional pricing that offers a discount on a product or service. They can be distributed through various channels such as newspapers, magazines, email, or social media. Coupons can be effective in attracting new customers and incentivising existing customers to make a purchase. For example, a restaurant might offer a coupon for a free appetiser or a percentage off the total bill.

- **Rebates:** A rebate is a discount given after purchase, often as cashback or a gift card. Rebates can incentivise customers to purchase a product or service and can encourage repeat business. For example, a computer manufacturer might offer a rebate after purchasing a new laptop for matching software or other related hardware.

- **Flash Sales:** Flash sales are time-limited promotions that offer a discount on a product or service for a short period, typically a few hours or a day. This type of promotional pricing can create a sense of urgency and encourage customers to purchase quickly. Flash sales are often used by eCommerce retailers such as Amazon or Zappos to clear out inventory or promote new products.

- **Volume Discounts:** Volume discounts are offered when a customer purchases large quantities of a product or service. This strategy is often used by wholesalers or manufacturers who sell to retailers. For example, a printer manufacturer might discount a company purchasing many printers.

How to Approach Price Wars

Price wars can emerge as a significant challenge for brands in the competitive business landscape. Engaging in a price war without a thoughtful strategy can harm a company's profitability and long-term success. Therefore, brands must adopt a prudent approach when confronted with pricing wars. This overview explores key insights and recommendations from the Harvard Business Review article 'How to Fight a Price War' by Akshay R. Rao and Mark E. Bergen (2000).

Price wars occur when competing brands engage in aggressive price reductions to gain market share or retaliate against a competitor's pricing strategy. Such wars often result in eroded profit margins and an unsustainable race to the bottom. However, brands can adopt effective strategies to navigate these turbulent waters and protect profitability.

Key Insights for Brands

Assess the Competitive Landscape: Brands should comprehensively analyse their competitors' strengths, weaknesses, and pricing strategies. Understanding market dynamics and customer preferences is essential in formulating a tailored response.

Determine Cost Advantage: It is crucial to ascertain whether a brand possesses a cost advantage over its competitors. Lowering prices without a sustainable cost advantage can be a risky move that may compromise profitability. Brands must create and leverage unique value propositions to justify the pricing.

Communicate Value Propositions: Rather than engaging solely in price reductions, brands should communicate their value propositions effectively. Highlighting product quality, superior customer service or unique features can differentiate the brand and justify a higher price point.

Monitor Customer Perceptions: Brands must continuously monitor customer perceptions and preferences to stay responsive to market demands. Gathering customer feedback and conducting market research can help identify areas for improvement and inform pricing decisions.

Consider Non-Price Competition: Brands should explore non-price strategies, such as product differentiation, innovation, or strategic partnerships, to gain a competitive edge. By offering unique and compelling experiences, brands can reduce their vulnerability to price-based competition.

Explore Pricing Segmentation: Adopting a segmented pricing strategy allows brands to tailor their offerings to different customer segments. By offering differentiated products or services, brands can capture value from customers willing to pay a premium for specific features.

Collaborate with Channel Partners: Brands should collaborate with channel partners, such as distributors or retailers, to ensure consistent pricing strategies and avoid destructive price wars. Aligning interests and fostering mutually beneficial relationships can help protect profitability.

Pricing is crucial to a company's financial health and brand perception.

See also:

Marketing Fundamentals: Marketing Ethics
Marketing Mix: Promotion
Market Analysis: Bowman's Strategic Clock
Market Analysis: Marketing Research
Consumer Behaviour: The Consumer Value Equation
Consumer Behaviour: Anchoring Bias

Chapter 20

Promotion

Promotion summarises all aspects to communicate with customers and persuade them to purchase a product or service. It encompasses the most 'visible' marketing activities, including advertising, personal selling, sales promotions, public relations, and direct marketing. Its goal within any marketing strategy is to help create brand awareness, build customer relationships, and drive sales.

The Types of Marketing Promotion

Advertising is one of the most widely used forms of promotion. It involves creating and placing advertisements in various media platforms such as print, television, radio, and online. Advertisements are designed to grab the attention of potential customers and communicate the features and benefits of a product or service. For example, Coca-Cola's 'Share a Coke' advert, promoted their personalised name bottles and cans to connect emotionally with customers and encourage them to buy and share the product with friends and families.

Personal selling involves a salesperson interacting with potential customers to persuade them to purchase a product or service. This form of promotion is more effective for products that require a higher level of personal attention or have a higher price point. For example, car dealerships often use personal selling techniques to help customers choose the right cars that meet their needs and budgets.

Sales promotion involves temporary incentives designed to encourage customers to make a purchase. Examples include coupons, discounts, free samples, and loyalty programs. Sales promotions can effectively increase short-term sales; however, incentives should not undermine the product's long-term value.

Public relations (PR) involves building positive relationships with the media and other stakeholders to create a positive image of a company or product. PR can include activities such as press releases, media events, and sponsorships. For example, Red Bull's 'Stratos' campaign involved sponsoring a daredevil who skydived from the edge of space, generating significant media coverage and enhancing the company's brand image.

Direct marketing involves communicating directly with individual customers through channels such as email, mail, or telemarketing. Direct marketing can be more targeted and cost-effective than other forms of promotion, but it is also important to ensure that the messages are relevant and not seen as spam. For example, Amazon uses personalised email recommendations based on customers' past purchases to encourage them to buy related products.

In later chapters, this book will detail some of the most common promotional formats with examples showing how businesses can design effective communication campaigns.

How to Choose the Right Promotional Strategy

In addition to these specific promotion methods, it is important to consider the overall promotion mix that will be most effective for a given product or service. It requires careful consideration of factors such as target audience, product features, competition, budget, and marketing objectives. Here are some steps businesses can follow to decide on the right promotional strategy for their business:

Understand the target audience: To develop an effective promotional strategy, businesses need to understand their target audience's needs, preferences, and behaviours. This information can be gathered through market research, surveys, focus groups, and social media analytics. Once businesses have clearly understood their target audience, they can tailor their promotional messages to resonate with them.

Define the marketing objectives: Businesses must define their objectives before selecting a promotional strategy. The objectives could be to increase brand awareness, generate leads, increase sales, or build customer loyalty. The promotional strategy should be aligned with the marketing objectives.

Analyse the competition: Businesses should analyse their competitors' promotional strategies to identify gaps and opportunities. They can evaluate the strengths and weaknesses of their competitors' promotional tactics and use this information to differentiate themselves from the competitors with their promotional strategy.

Determine the budget: The promotional strategy should be within the business's budget. Businesses should determine how much they can afford to spend on promotional activities and allocate the budget accordingly. They should also consider the return on investment (aka. ROI) of each promotional tactic and choose the ones that offer the highest ROI.

Evaluate the effectiveness: Once the promotional strategy is implemented, businesses should track and evaluate its effectiveness. They can use such metrics such as website traffic, social media engagement, lead conversion rates, and sales revenue to measure the impact of the promotional strategy. Businesses can adjust their promotional strategy based on the results to improve their effectiveness.

Promotion is often the first part of the marketing mix customers see.

See also:

Marketing Mix: Price
Consumer Behaviour: Anchoring Bias
Marketing Communication: Advertising Types by Objective
Marketing Communication: Copywriting
Marketing Communication: TV Advertising
Marketing Communication: Print Advertising
Marketing Communication: Radio Advertising
Marketing Communication: Out-of-Home Advertising
Marketing Communication: Public Relations
Marketing Communication: Word-of-Mouth Advertising
Marketing Communication: Influencer Marketing
Marketing Communication: Email Marketing
Marketing Communication: Pay-per-Click Advertising

Chapter 21

Place

The place element of the marketing mix, or distribution, refers to the methods and channels that businesses use to make their products or services available to customers. This element is crucial to a business's marketing strategy in light of the fact that it determines how effectively it can reach its target audience and deliver its product or service. In this chapter, we will explore the importance of the place element of the marketing mix and provide examples of businesses that have successfully implemented effective distribution strategies into the market.

The Importance of Place

The place element of the marketing mix is important because it directly enables companies to reach their target audiences and generate sales. A poorly planned distribution strategy can result in low sales and limited market share, while an effective strategy can lead to increased sales and a stronger market position.

Accessibility: Customers need to access a product or service to purchase it easily. A business's distribution strategy must consider location, transportation, and convenience to ensure customers can access their product or service.

Efficiency: An effective distribution strategy should also be efficient, minimising the costs associated with delivering a product or service to customers. This can include transportation costs, inventory management, and order processing.

Competitive Advantage: The distribution strategy can also provide a competitive advantage for a business by allowing them to reach its target audience more effectively than its competitors. This can include faster delivery times, more convenient locations, and a wider range of distribution channels.

Brand Image: The distribution strategy can also affect a business's brand image by shaping the customer's perception of the company. For example, a business that uses high-end retail stores to distribute its products will likely be perceived as more upscale and premium than a business that uses discount retailers.

Distribution Channels To Consider

There are various distribution channels for services and products across different types of businesses.

- **Direct selling:** Businesses can sell their products or services directly to customers through various methods such as door-to-door sales, telemarketing, direct mail, or vending machines.

- **Retail stores:** Physical retail stores provide a traditional distribution channel for businesses to sell their products. This can include company-owned stores or franchise-owned stores.

- **Online marketplaces:** Businesses can leverage online marketplaces including Amazon, eBay, Coupang, or Etsy to sell their products directly to customers.

- **eCommerce websites:** Companies can create eCommerce websites to sell their products and services directly to customers. These websites can be either company-owned or third-party hosted.

- **Social media:** Social media platforms like Facebook, Instagram, and Twitter provide a platform for businesses to showcase their products and services and sell directly to customers through their pages and profiles.

- **Wholesalers and distributors:** Businesses can use wholesalers and distributors to distribute their products and services to retailers or other businesses.

- **Subscription services:** Businesses can offer subscription-based services to customers, providing regular access to their products or services.

The choice of distribution channel(s) depends on factors such as the type of product or service, target audience, and budget. Some businesses may use a combination of distribution channels to reach a wider audience and maximise sales. This book explores some of these channels in more detail later on.

Channel Strategies

There are various distribution channel strategies that businesses can choose from, including:

- **Direct distribution:** This involves selling products directly to customers without any intermediaries. This can be done through company-owned stores, eCommerce websites, or direct mail.

- **Indirect distribution:** This involves using intermediaries such as wholesalers, distributors, or retailers to sell products to customers. This is a common strategy used by many businesses to reach a broader customer base and increase the availability of their products.

- **Multichannel distribution:** This involves using multiple distribution channels to reach customers, such as a combination of company-owned stores, eCommerce websites, and third-party retailers.

- **Exclusive distribution:** This involves limiting the number of retailers allowed to sell a product, usually by entering into exclusive contracts with specific retailers. This is often used for luxury brands or high-end products.

- **Selective distribution:** This involves using a limited number of retailers to sell a product, usually based on specific criteria such as geographic location or market segment. This is often used for products that require specialised knowledge or expertise to sell.

In addition to choosing a distribution channel strategy, businesses must consider logistics, inventory management, and order fulfilment when developing their place strategy.

Examples of Effective Distribution Strategies

Apple: Apple's distribution strategy is focused on creating an immersive retail experience that reflects its brand image. They achieve this through their flagship stores, designed to be visually striking and highly interactive. By providing a unique in-store experience, Apple can differentiate itself from competitors and reinforce its brand identity.

Coca-Cola: Coca-Cola's highly effective distribution strategy allows them to reach customers in almost every corner of the world. They achieve this by partnering with local bottling companies to produce and distribute their products. This approach allows them to adapt to local market conditions and preferences while maintaining a consistent brand image.

Amazon: Amazon's distribution strategy is centred around speed and convenience. They achieve this through their vast network of fulfilment centres, partnerships with shipping providers, and investment in new technologies such as drones and autonomous vehicles. By offering fast and reliable delivery, Amazon has become a go-to source for online shopping.

Nike: Nike's distribution strategy focuses on a multichannel approach that allows them to reach customers through its retail stores, online marketplaces, and partnerships with third-party retailers. This approach allows them to reach customers in various ways and provide a seamless shopping experience across all channels.

Place focuses on how businesses can effectively reach their target audience and deliver their product or service.

See also:

Product Distribution: Brick & Mortar Retail Stores
Product Distribution: Online Marketplace
Product Distribution: eCommerce

Chapter 22

People

One of the essential components of marketing is the people element. Marketing is about creating value for customers and delivering it in a way that satisfies their needs and wants. People in this framework refers to both the people buying and selling the product or service. In this chapter we will focus on all individuals involved in creating and delivering a product or service, including employees, managers, and executives. For more information on consumers, please refer to the 'Consumer Profiling' chapter in Marketing Fundamentals.

The Role of People

The people element of the marketing mix plays an essential role in achieving a company's marketing objectives. The quality of personnel and their abilities can significantly impact the customer's perception of the product or service; the customer experience; and, ultimately, the company's success. A company's employees are the face of the organisation and are responsible for delivering the company's value proposition to customers. In other words, they are the key to building and maintaining a solid brand image.

The people element of the marketing mix involves several key areas, including recruitment, training, motivation, and customer service.

Recruitment is central when it comes to ensuring the company that has the right people in the correct positions to achieve its marketing objectives. Hiring the right personnel with the right skills, knowledge, and experience can help a company differentiate itself from its competitors and create a competitive advantage. Training is also imperative when it comes to ensuring that employees have the necessary skills and knowledge to perform their jobs effectively. Investing in employee training and development can increase employee engagement, motivation, and job satisfaction, resulting in better customer service and higher customer satisfaction.

Motivation is another factor in the people element of the marketing mix. Motivated employees are more productive, engaged, and committed to achieving the company's goals. Companies can motivate their employees by providing a positive work environment, offering competitive compensation and benefits packages, recognising and rewarding employee achievements, and offering opportunities for career advancement.

Customer service is the final aspect of the people element of the marketing mix. It can significantly impact the customer's perception of the product or service and influence their purchasing decisions. Providing exceptional customer service can build customer loyalty, increase customer satisfaction, and generate positive word-of-mouth advertising.

Examples of People in Marketing Strategy

There are numerous examples of how companies have used the people element of the marketing mix to achieve success.

Zappos is an online retailer known for its exceptional customer service. They invest heavily in employee training and development to ensure their employees have the skills and knowledge necessary. Zappos also has a policy of offering a 365-day return policy on all products, which demonstrates its commitment to customer satisfaction.

Apple is a company known for its strong company culture and a reputation for innovation. It invests heavily in employee training and development to ensure that its employees have the skills and knowledge necessary to create innovative products. Their retail stores are known for their exceptional customer service, and employees are trained to provide a personalised and engaging customer experience. Employees are also trained to upsell and cross-sell products, which helps to increase sales and generate more revenue for the company.

Starbucks is another example of a company that has used the people element of the marketing mix to achieve success. Starbucks invests heavily in employee training and development to ensure its employees have the skills and knowledge to create the perfect cup of coffee. They also have a policy of treating its employees well, offering competitive compensation and benefits packages, and providing opportunities for career advancement. This approach has helped Starbucks to build a strong company culture, increase employee engagement and motivation, and provide exceptional customer service.

In the People section of the marketing mix, we focus on who will sell and buy the product.

See also:

Marketing Fundamentals: What is Marketing?
Marketing Fundamentals: Consumer Profiling
Marketing Mix: The 6P Framework

Chapter 23

Process

The marketing mix is a fundamental concept in the business world, which involves combining various elements to create a successful marketing strategy. The five fundamental aspects of the marketing mix are product, people, price, place, and promotion. However, the process is a sixth aspect of the marketing mix that is often overlooked but equally essential. Here, we will explore the process aspect of the marketing mix, which is concerned with delivering a product or service to the target customers.

Process in Marketing

Process refers to an organisation's activities to provide a product or service to its customers. It involves everything from ordering, manufacturing, packaging, and delivering the product or service to the customer. The process is essential to the marketing mix because it ensures customer satisfaction. A good process ensures that customers receive their products or services promptly and efficiently, which can lead to increased customer loyalty and repeat business.

Process in Service Marketing

The process is particularly critical in the service industry because services are intangible and cannot be touched or seen. Therefore, the process is often the only tangible evidence customers have of the service. Delivering a service can influence the customer's perception of the service quality and affect the customer's satisfaction with the service.

For example, consider a restaurant with excellent food but poor service. Customers perceiving poor treatment can find their dining experience ruined, even if the food is great. Therefore, ensuring that the service-delivery process is efficient and effective is essential.

Process in Product Marketing

Similarly, the process can also influence product quality perception regarding physical products. For example, if a customer orders a product online and takes a long time to arrive, the customer may perceive the company or product as lower quality, even if that's not the case. Therefore, companies selling physical goods should consider the entire journey from manufacturing to delivery as part of the consumer experience.

Process Mapping

Mapping is a tool businesses use to analyse and improve their processes. It involves visualising a process to identify its steps, inputs, outputs, and stakeholders. Process mapping helps companies to understand how a process works, how long it takes, and what issues might be present. It also provides a clear picture of the process flow and the stakeholders' roles. Businesses can use process mapping in several ways.

First, it can be used to improve customer service. By mapping the customer service process, companies can identify areas where customers experience delays or frustration. This can help companies to improve their customer service experience and increase customer satisfaction.

Second, mapping can be used to improve manufacturing processes. By visualising the manufacturing process, businesses can identify areas where waste occurs or where there are inefficiencies. This can help companies to reduce costs and increase productivity.

Third, process mapping can be used to improve information technology processes. By mapping the IT process, businesses can identify areas where systems need to be integrated or manual processes occur. This can help companies to streamline their IT processes, reduce errors, and increase productivity.

To use process mapping, companies should follow a few key steps. First, they should identify the process that they want to map. This could be a customer service process, a manufacturing process, or an IT process. Second, they should create a visual representation of the process flow. This can be done using flowcharts, swim lane diagrams, or process maps. Third, they should identify the stakeholders involved in the process and their roles. Finally, they should analyse the process flow and identify areas for improvement.

Process Improvement

Process improvement is a critical aspect of any successful business, and it involves identifying and eliminating inefficiencies in business processes. While many companies focus on improving the most visible and high-impact processes, several common areas for process improvement should be addressed. Here are some examples:

Communication: Poor communication is one of the most common areas for process improvement. This can include a need for more communication between teams, unclear communication, or miscommunication. Improving communication can ensure everyone is on the same page, reduce the risk of errors, and speed up processes.

Standardisation: Standardizing processes is an effective way to increase efficiency and reduce errors. However, many businesses need to pay more attention to the benefits of standardisation and continue to use ad-hoc processes that are not standardised across different teams or departments.

Training: Training employees can help improve processes and reduce errors. Many businesses assume employees are already familiar with the processes they must perform, but this is often different. Training on new processes or technologies can help reduce errors and increase productivity.

Automation: Automation is another area for process improvement that needs to be addressed. Automating manual processes can reduce errors, speed up processes, and increase productivity. However, many businesses are hesitant to invest in automation due to concerns about cost or a need to understand how automation can benefit their business.

Feedback: Collecting feedback from customers, employees, or other stakeholders is essential for improving processes. However, many companies need to pay more attention to the importance of feedback and collect it consistently or effectively.

A good process ensures that customers receive their products or services promptly and efficiently, which can lead to increased customer loyalty and repeat business.

See also:

Marketing Measurement: Key Performance Indicators

V

Consumer Behaviour

Chapter 24

Behavioural Psychology in Marketing

The field of marketing is all about understanding and influencing human behaviours. As the scientific study of human behaviour and mental processes, psychology provides marketers with valuable insights into how people think, feel, and make decisions. Both fields are so interconnected that marketers must understand basic consumer behaviour concepts if they seek mastery as it provides insights into customers' preferences, motivations, and needs. Here, we will discuss the importance of consumer behaviour in marketing and its essential components.

The Importance of Consumer Behaviours in Marketing

Understanding Customer Needs and Preferences

This understanding allows marketers to develop products and services that meet the needs of their customers, increasing the chances of success in the market. By analysing consumer behaviour, marketers can identify gaps in the market, opportunities for growth, and potential areas for product development.

Creating Effective Marketing Strategies

Consumer behaviour insights enable marketers to create effective marketing strategies that resonate with their target audience. By understanding what motivates customers to purchase products and services, marketers can tailor their marketing messages to appeal to the needs and wants of their customers. This helps build trust and loyalty, increasing the likelihood of repeat purchases and positive word-of-mouth recommendations.

Improving Customer Experience

By analysing customer behaviour, marketers can identify pain points and areas for improvement in the customer journey. This allows marketers to create a better overall customer experience, increasing customer satisfaction and loyalty.

Components of Consumer Behaviours

Personal Factors

Personal factors refer to the characteristics of an individual that influence their behaviour, such as age, gender, income, education, and personality. These factors influence how consumers perceive products and services, and impact decision-making.

Psychological Factors

Psychological factors are the mental processes influencing consumer behaviour, such as motivation, perception, learning, and attitudes. These factors play a critical role in shaping consumer behaviours and decision-making processes. For example, a consumer who is motivated to stay healthy may be more likely to purchase organic or healthy food products.

Social Factors

Social factors refer to the influence of family, friends, and other social groups on consumer behaviour. The elements can impact consumer behaviour in several ways, such as shaping preferences and influencing purchasing decisions. For example, a consumer may be more likely to purchase a product if a friend or family member recommends it.

Cultural Factors

Cultural factors refer to the impact of culture on consumer behaviours. These factors include values, beliefs, customs, and traditions, influencing how consumers perceive and evaluate products and services. Cultural factors can also impact decision-making, as consumers may be more likely to purchase products that align with their cultural values.

Situational Factors

Situational factors refer to the context in which a consumer makes a purchase. This can include time, place, and other environmental factors that impact the decision-making process. For example, a consumer may be more likely to purchase a product if it is easily accessible and convenient.

Applications in Marketing

Target Audience

Understanding consumer behaviours helps marketers identify their target audience and develop marketing strategies that resonate with that audience. For example, a luxury watch company may target wealthy consumers who value quality and exclusivity.

Product Development

If wanting to sell athletic shoes, a company may research what features and designs are most important to their customers, and then use this information to develop products that meet those needs.

Pricing Strategy

As humans, we're hardwired to evaluate and compare options constantly. For example, a company that targets budget-conscious consumers may use pricing strategies such as discounts or promotions to attract customers. On the other hand, a luxury brand may use premium pricing to appeal to consumers who value exclusivity and high-end products.

Advertising and Promotion

By understanding the values and motivations of their target audience, marketers can create advertising messages that resonate with consumers. For example, a company that sells environmentally friendly products may use messaging that emphasises the benefits of sustainable living.

Customer Experience

Finally, companies can identify pain points in the customer journey by analysing customer behaviour and improving customer satisfaction. For example, a retailer may improve their online checkout process to make it more user-friendly and reduce cart abandonment rates.

Customer behaviour is likely to change over time, so it is vital to understand current trends and predict future market trends.

Consumer behaviour provides insights into customers' needs, preferences, and motivations.

See also:

Marketing Fundamentals: Consumer Profiling
Marketing Fundamentals: Marketing Research
Marketing Mix: Product
Marketing Mix: Price
Marketing Mix: Promotion
Consumer Behaviour: The Consumer Value Equation

Chapter 25

Consumer Value Equation

The Consumer Value Equation is a marketing concept used for decades to help businesses understand how consumers perceive value and make purchasing decisions. The equation has its roots in the early 20th century, when economists began studying consumer behaviours and the factors influencing purchasing decisions. In this chapter, we will explore the history of the Consumer Value Equation, provide a detailed description of its components, and discuss how businesses can use it to inform their marketing strategies.

History of the Consumer Value Equation

The concept can be traced back to the early 20th century, when economists began to study consumer behaviours in more detail. One of the earliest studies on this topic was conducted by the American economist John Bates Clark. In 1899, he suggested that the value of a product or service was determined by the marginal utility it provided to the consumer. This theory was later refined by other economists, such as Irving Fisher and Vilfredo Pareto, who developed more sophisticated models of consumer behaviours.

In the mid-20th century, marketing researchers focused on the psychological factors influencing consumer behaviours, such as perceptions of quality, price, and value. One of the most influential researchers in this area was Philip Kotler, who first introduced the concept of the Consumer Value Equation in his book *Marketing Management* in 1967. Kotler defined the equation as follows:

Value = Benefits / Price

This suggests that consumers perceive value based on the ratio of benefits to price. In other words, if the benefits of a product or service outweigh its price, then consumers will perceive it as having high value. If the price is too high relative to the benefits, consumers will perceive it as having low value.

Components of the Consumer Value Equation

Let's take a closer look at the equation's two components: value and price.

Benefits refer to a product's or service's positive attributes or features that consumers value. These can include functional benefits, such as convenience, reliability, or performance, and emotional benefits, such as status, satisfaction, or enjoyment. Benefits can also be tangible or intangible and vary depending on the consumer's needs and preferences.

Price refers to the cost of a product or service, including any monetary or non-monetary sacrifices consumers must make to acquire it. This can include the purchase price and associated costs, such as shipping, installation, or maintenance. Price can also be influenced by factors such as discounts, promotions, or perceived value.

Using the Consumer Value Equation in Marketing Strategy

Understanding the Consumer Value Equation can be extremely valuable for businesses looking to develop effective marketing strategies. By focusing on the benefits of their products or services and finding ways to increase perceived value, businesses can attract and retain customers, differentiate themselves from competitors, and ultimately increase sales and profits.

- **Emphasise benefits:** One of the most important ways to increase perceived value is to emphasise a product's or service's benefits. This can be done through advertising, packaging, or other forms of promotion. By highlighting the positive attributes of a product or service, a business can make it more attractive to consumers and increase its perceived value.

- **Optimise pricing:** Another key strategy is to optimise pricing to maximise perceived value. This can involve adjusting prices based on market conditions, offering discounts or promotions, or using psychological pricing tactics to make prices more appealing. By finding the right price point, businesses can ensure that consumers perceive their products or services as having high value.

- **Focus on customer needs:** Ultimately, the key to success with the Consumer Value Equation is to focus on the needs and preferences of the target audience. By understanding what benefits are most important to consumers and how they perceive price, businesses can tailor their marketing strategies to meet their needs better. This can involve conducting market research, analysing consumer data, and developing customer personas to understand the target audience better.

- **Differentiate from competitors:** Another important aspect of using the Consumer Value Equation in marketing is differentiation. By emphasising unique benefits and features that set their products or services apart from competitors, businesses can increase perceived value and attract customers looking for something different. This can involve developing unique branding, offering innovative features, or providing exceptional customer service.

- **Monitor and adjust:** Finally, it's important to continually monitor and adjust marketing strategies based on consumer feedback and changing market conditions. By staying current on trends and consumer preferences, businesses can ensure that they provide the best possible value to their customers and remain competitive in the marketplace.

Limitations of the Framework

While the Consumer Value Equation is a useful framework for understanding how consumers perceive value and make purchasing decisions, it does have some limitations. It's important for businesses to be aware of these limitations and to use the equation as a guide rather than a rigid set of rules.

- **It doesn't account for emotional factors:** The Equation focuses on the rational, economic factors influencing purchasing decisions, such as price and benefits. However, consumers are also influenced by emotional factors such as brand perception, social proof, and personal preferences. In addition, benefits are sometimes hard to qualify and might not hold the same value for all users. Businesses should be aware of these factors and account for them in their marketing strategies.

- **It assumes consumers are rational:** While the Consumer Value Equation assumes that consumers make purchasing decisions based on rational considerations, consumers are often influenced by subconscious biases and emotions. For example, a consumer might be willing to pay more for a product simply because it has a prestigious brand name, even if the benefits are the same as a cheaper product.

- **It doesn't account for cultural differences:** The Consumer Value Equation assumes that all consumers value benefits and prices similarly. However, cultural differences can significantly impact how consumers perceive value. For example, haggling over price in some cultures is common, while it's considered rude in others. Businesses operating in different cultural contexts should be aware of these differences and adjust their marketing strategies accordingly.

- **It doesn't account for changing consumer preferences:** Consumer preferences are constantly changing. What consumers value today may not be the same as what they value tomorrow. Businesses must stay current on changing trends and consumer preferences, and adjust their marketing strategies accordingly.

- **It doesn't account for competitive factors:** While the Consumer Value Equation can help businesses differentiate themselves from competitors by emphasising unique benefits and features, it doesn't account for the competitive landscape. Businesses must be aware of their competitor's marketing strategies and adjust them accordingly.

The Consumer Value helps businesses understand how consumers perceive value and make purchasing decisions.

See also:

Brand Building: Brand Positioning
The Marketing Mix: Price
Consumer Behaviour: Anchoring Bias

Chapter 26

Anchoring Bias

Anchoring bias is a cognitive bias that affects people's decision-making process. It refers to the tendency to rely too heavily on the first piece of information (the anchor) presented when making decisions. This bias can lead to errors in judgment and decision-making. In marketing, anchoring bias influences consumers' perceptions of pricing and value. Once an anchor has been established, people tend to make judgments or decisions based on that initial information, even if it is irrelevant or inaccurate.

Why does it work?

Research suggests that the anchoring bias takes advantage of how the human brain processes information and makes decisions. When individuals encounter an anchor, it can serve as a mental reference point that influences their perception of subsequent information. The initial anchor can influence people's thoughts, attitudes, and beliefs, leading them to adjust their judgments or decisions based on this reference point.

Furthermore, the anchoring bias may also be influenced by individuals' reliance on heuristics, which are mental shortcuts that people use to simplify decision-making. When faced with complex decisions, the anchor may act as a heuristic that helps individuals make quicker and easier judgments without thoroughly evaluating all relevant information.

Another factor is that the anchoring bias may tap into individuals' natural tendency to seek confirmation for their beliefs or preconceived notions. Once an anchor is established, individuals may selectively interpret or perceive the following information in a way that confirms or aligns with the anchor, leading to biased judgments or decisions.

Social and cultural factors may also play a role in anchoring bias. Social pressure, conformity, and the desire to be consistent with others may lead individuals to rely on anchors provided by authority figures, peers, or societal norms, even if they are not objectively relevant to the decision.

Application of Anchoring Bias in Marketing

Anchoring bias is commonly used to influence consumers' perceptions of pricing and value. Marketers often use anchoring bias to their advantage by presenting an initial piece of information that sets the tone for subsequent decision-making. This initial piece of information is often a price point or value proposition.

Pricing

Anchoring bias is commonly used in pricing strategies. For example, a company may offer a high-priced product for a period to create an anchor point and then lower the price for certain days to suggest better value. The lower-priced product is more attractive to consumers because it is compared to the higher-priced product, making them believe that they are getting a better deal when in reality, the initial price might have been heavily overestimated.

Value

Anchoring bias can also influence consumers' perceptions of value. For example, a company may offer a product that is priced high but has additional features or benefits not offered by competitors. By comparing features between competitive products, consumers may perceive the product as higher quality or more valuable.

While anchoring bias can be an effective marketing strategy, it is essential to be aware of its limitations. One limitation is that the anchor must be relevant to the decision. If the anchor is not applicable, it may not influence subsequent decision-making. Another limitation is that the anchor must be presented in a way that is perceived as credible. If the anchor is not perceived as credible, it may not influence decision-making.

Examples of Using the Anchoring Bias

When shopping for a streaming service, a customer has three options: a basic plan for £8 per month, a standard plan for £12 per month, and a premium plan for £16 per month. The basic plan seems too limited for their needs, while the premium plan seems too expensive. The customer may choose the standard plan, which balances price and features well.

This phenomenon is known as the 'decoy effect' or the 'asymmetric dominance effect'. and takes advantage of our anchoring bias. The high- and low-priced options are strategically placed to influence customers to choose the 'golden middle' and move customers away from the cheapest option. In the long-term, this also allows the company to be more flexible in case customers want to switch levels by having the option to move them to a cheaper tier rather, than lose them completely.

Anchoring bias can influence consumers' perceptions of pricing and value.

See also:

Brand Building: Brand Positioning
Marketing Mix: Price
Marketing Mix: Promotion
Consumer Behaviour: Consumer Value Equation

Chapter 27

Social Proof

The concept of social proof is a powerful psychological phenomenon that plays a vital role in human decision-making. It refers to the tendency to look to others when making decisions or taking action, especially in situations where we are uncertain or unsure of what to do. In marketing, social proof can influence consumer behaviours and drive sales. This section will explore the concept of social proof in behavioural psychology, examine its different forms, and consider how it can be applied in marketing, looking at case studies.

What is Social Proof, and Why does it work?

Social Proof is a cognitive shortcut that allows us to make decisions quickly and with minimal effort. When we see others doing something, we assume it is the right thing to do and follow suit. This phenomenon is especially true when we are unsure of what to do or where the stakes are high.

- **Conformity:** Humans naturally tend to conform to social norms and align their behaviours with those of others. When people see others engaging, they are more likely to follow suit to fit in and be accepted by the group. This is especially true when appropriate behaviours are unclear or ambiguous.

- **Trust and credibility:** Social proof can also enhance trust and credibility. When people see others endorsing a product or service, they are more likely to trust it as reliable and of high quality. People often assume that if others use or endorse a product, it must be good or worthwhile.

- **Emotional contagion:** Social proof can also work through emotional contagion, where the emotions of others influence people's emotions. When people see others expressing positive emotions towards a product or service, they are more likely to experience similar emotions, leading them to view the product or service more positively.

Types of Social Proof

Expert Social Proof

Expert social proof is when an authority figure or expert in a particular field endorses a product or service. This type of social proof is effective because it suggests that the product or service has been vetted by someone who knows what they are discussing. For example, a dentist endorsing a particular brand of toothpaste or a fitness coach promoting a weight loss program.

Celebrity Social Proof

Celebrity social proof is when a well-known public figure endorses a product or service. This type of social proof can be very effective because people often look up to celebrities and want to emulate their behaviours. Examples are Michael Jordan endorsing Nike shoes or the Kardashians promoting anything.

User Social Proof

User social proof is when a product or service is endorsed by its users. This type of social proof is effective because it suggests that the product or service has been tried and tested by others and found to be satisfactory. Examples include customer testimonials, reviews, and ratings.

Wisdom of the Crowd Social Proof

Wisdom of the crowd social proof is when a large group endorses a product or service. This type of social proof is effective because it suggests that the product or service is popular and widely accepted. Examples include social media likes, followers, or online trends such as #tiktokmademebuyit.

Application of Social Proof in Marketing

Social proof can be used in marketing to influence consumer behaviour and drive sales. Here are some examples of how social proof can be applied in marketing:

Customer Testimonials

One of the most common ways to use social proof in marketing is through customer testimonials. By featuring positive feedback from satisfied customers, businesses can show potential customers that their product or service is influential and trustworthy. Testimonials can be displayed on a website, social media page, or in advertising materials.

Expert Endorsements

Expert endorsements are another effective way to use social proof in marketing. Businesses can leverage the expert's reputation to build trust and credibility. This can be done through sponsorships, partnerships, or by featuring quotes or endorsements on advertising materials.

Social Media Influencers

Social media influencers are a popular way to utilise this behavioural trait for business. Influencers have built large followings on social media platforms and can influence the behaviours of their followers. By partnering with an influencer with a large following in a particular niche, businesses can reach a wider audience and increase their credibility.

User-Generated Content

User-generated content is another effective way to use social proof in marketing. By encouraging customers to share their experiences with a product or service on social media platforms, businesses can create a sense of community and build trust with potential customers.

While social proof can do a lot of good, it is important to note that it can also negatively impact a business. For example, poor customer reviews or ratings can significantly impact sales. Additionally, a company must rely only on more than just social proof, as this may come across as inauthentic or manipulative.

By leveraging the power of social proof, businesses can build trust with their customers and increase their sales.

See also:

Marketing Communication: Influencer Marketing
Marketing Distribution: Online Marketplace

Chapter 28

The Paradox of Choice

The paradox of choice is a phenomenon in behavioural psychology suggesting that too many options can decrease satisfaction and increase anxiety. The idea is that when people are faced with too many choices, they become overwhelmed and cannot decide at all. This so-called 'freeze' can lead to regret and dissatisfaction, even if a decision is eventually made. In marketing, the paradox of choice has important implications for product design, pricing strategies, and consumer behaviours.

Why does it work?

Decision paralysis: When consumers are presented with too many options, it can lead to decision paralysis, where they become overwhelmed and find it difficult to make a choice. This can happen because the cognitive effort required to evaluate numerous options becomes mentally taxing, and consumers may worry about making the wrong decision or missing out on a better option. As a result, they may delay or avoid making a decision altogether, leading to lost sales or missed opportunities for marketers.

Regret and dissatisfaction: The paradox of choice can also lead to post-decision regret and dissatisfaction. When consumers have many options to choose from and finally decide, they may experience regret or second-guess their choice, wondering if another option would have been better. This can diminish their satisfaction with the chosen option and result in negative feelings towards the overall decision-making process or the brand, potentially reducing customer loyalty.

Simplification and heuristics: In the face of many options, consumers may resort to simplification strategies and heuristics to make decisions more manageable. For example, they may rely on brand familiarity, price, or other simple decision rules to quickly narrow down their options. This can result in consumers making suboptimal choices or relying on biases and heuristics that may not always lead to the best outcomes.

Applications in Marketing

Product assortment: Marketers often face the challenge of deciding how many options to offer in a product assortment. While having a wide range of options may seem appealing, it can overwhelm consumers and lead to decision paralysis. By carefully curating and limiting the number of choices, marketers can help consumers make more confident and satisfying decisions.

Pricing and promotions: More or more complex pricing options can complicate consumer decision-making. Marketers can use the paradox of choice to simplify pricing structures or promotions, making them easier to understand and choose from. For example, offering simple pricing tiers or promotional packages instead of many complex options can help consumers make decisions more quickly.

Website design and user experience: Website design and user experience play a crucial role in eCommerce and online marketing. A website with complex navigation options, buttons, or choices can overwhelm visitors and lower engagement and conversion rates. Applying the principles of the paradox of choice, marketers can simplify website design, streamline navigation, and reduce the number of options presented to visitors, making the website more user-friendly and effective.

Recommendations and personalisation: Marketers often use recommendation engines and personalisation techniques to provide customised options to consumers based on their preferences and behaviours. However, if the recommendations are overly complex or overwhelming, consumers may feel burdened by too many choices. By applying the paradox of choice, marketers can optimise recommendation algorithms and personalisation strategies to balance customisation and simplicity, making it easier for consumers to make decisions.

Marketing campaigns: In marketing campaigns, too much information, too many offers, or too many calls to action can dilute the campaign's effectiveness. Applying the paradox of choice, marketers can simplify their messaging, focus on a few key offers, and provide clear and concise calls to action to avoid overwhelming consumers and increase the chances of desired consumer responses.

The Paradox of Choice in Practice

One of the most well-known examples of the paradox of choice in marketing comes from the world of consumer electronics. In the early 2000s, electronics retailer Best Buy noticed that customers were overwhelmed by the many options available in their stores. In response, the company streamlined its product offerings and focused on offering fewer products. This strategy succeeded, and Best Buy saw increased sales and customer satisfaction.

Another example of the paradox of choice in marketing comes from online dating. A study published in Cyberpsychology found that online daters were more satisfied with their choices when presented with fewer potential matches. Specifically, the study found that daters given a choice of three possible matches were more confident than those who chose 24 possible matches.

Another example is the success of Apple's product line. Although Apple offers fewer product options than many competitors, its simple and streamlined product line has helped establish the brand as a leader in the tech industry.

Subscription services have also taken advantage of this paradox. Netflix and Amazon Prime offer a wide variety of movies, TV shows, and other content, but the user interface is designed to make it easy for users to find something to watch. By curating content and offering personalised recommendations, these services reduce the indecisiveness that can come from having too many options.

Marketers can take several steps to avoid the adverse effects of the Paradox of Choice. First, they can limit the options available to consumers, focusing on the most popular or highest-quality products. They can also make decision-making easier by providing precise and concise information about each product, including its features, benefits, and price. Additionally, they can offer personalised recommendations based on a consumer's past behaviours or preferences.

Simplify the decision-making process for consumers, to increase sales and customer satisfaction.

See also:

Marketing Mix: Price
Marketing Mix: Promotion
Marketing Mix: Place
Product Distribution: Brick & Mortar Retail Stores
Product Distribution: Online Marketplace
Product Distribution: eCommerce

Chapter 29

The Reciprocity Effect

The reciprocity effect is a social psychology principle that shows people tend to respond to kind and generous actions with similar behaviours. In other words, if someone does something nice for us, we are more likely to feel obligated to reciprocate that kindness. This principle works on people because humans desire to balance social exchanges and avoid feeling indebted to others.

Application in Marketing

The reciprocity effect is a powerful principle with significant applications in marketing. By understanding and leveraging this principle, businesses can increase customer loyalty, build brand trust, and generate more sales. Here are some possible applications, along with examples:

Free samples or trials: Offering free samples or trials of a product is a common way to leverage the reciprocity effect. By giving customers a taste of the product, businesses hope to generate a sense of obligation to reciprocate the favour by purchasing the product. For example, a local cheese vendor at a local market might offer small bites of their product to get visitors to stop for a moment and entice them to make a purchase.

Gifts and incentives: Giving gifts or incentives to customers is another way to leverage the reciprocity effect. By providing customers with something of value, businesses hope to generate a sense of obligation to return the favour through purchases or other actions. For example, an online retailer may offer a gift with a purchase of a certain value, hoping to incentivise the customer to make larger purchases in the future.

Personalised messages and experiences: Personalisation is a powerful marketing technique that can leverage reciprocity. By providing personalised messages or experiences to customers, businesses can feel obligated to reciprocate the effort by purchasing or sharing their experience with others. For example, a travel company may personalise their marketing messages based on the customer's travel history or preferences, hoping to generate a sense of loyalty and increase the likelihood of future bookings.

Social responsibility and charitable initiatives: Companies that engage in social responsibility and charitable initiatives can also leverage the reciprocity effect. By doing good deeds, businesses can generate a sense of goodwill and obligation in their customers, who may be more likely to support the business. For example, a clothing company may donate a portion of their profits to a charitable cause, hoping to generate a sense of obligation among its customers to support the cause and the company.

How to Leverage the Effect

- **Perceived sincerity:** The perceived sincerity of the initial act of kindness can influence the strength of the reciprocity effect. If the act is seen as genuine and authentic, the recipient is more likely to feel obligated to reciprocate.

- **Timing:** The timing of the initial act of kindness can also impact the strength of the reciprocity effect. If the act occurs when the recipient is in need or under stress, they may feel a stronger obligation to reciprocate.

- **Personalisation:** Personalising the initial act of kindness can also increase the strength of the reciprocity effect. If the act is tailored to the recipient's preferences or needs, they may feel a stronger obligation to reciprocate.

- **Size and value of the initial act:** The size and value of the initial act of kindness can impact the strength of the reciprocity effect. The recipient may feel a stronger obligation to reciprocate if the act is significant and valuable.

- **Relationship between the giver and receiver:** The relationship between the giver and receiver can also impact the strength of the reciprocity effect. If the two parties have a close or positive relationship, the recipient may feel a stronger obligation to reciprocate.

- **Culture and social norms:** Cultural and social norms can also influence the strength of the reciprocity effect. In some cultures, reciprocity is highly valued and expected, while it may not be as crucial in others.

Limitations of the Effect in Practice

While the reciprocity effect can be a powerful tool in marketing, it is essential to use it ethically and avoid manipulating customers into feeling obligated. Here are some limitations and bad examples of the reciprocity effect being used in business:

- **Deceptive tactics:** Using deceptive tactics to exploit the reciprocity effect is unethical and can damage the reputation of a business. For example, a company that offers a gift with a purchase but then requires the customer to pay for shipping or handling may leave the customer feeling deceived and less likely to make a repeat purchase.

- **Overuse:** Overusing the reciprocity effect can lead to customer fatigue and a loss of trust in a business. For example, a company constantly bombards its customers with promotional offers or free samples that may be seen as insincere and lose credibility.

- **Inappropriate timing:** Using the reciprocity effect at inappropriate times can backfire and damage customer relationships. For example, a company that offers a gift or incentive in exchange for a positive review may be seen as manipulative and damage customers' trust.

- **Lack of authenticity:** The reciprocity effect only works when customers perceive the actions of a business as genuine and sincere. If a business's actions appear inauthentic or insincere, customers may not feel obligated to reciprocate. For example, a company that donates to a charity as a publicity stunt may not rate the difference of obligation that genuinely supports a charitable cause.

Understanding the reciprocity effect will lead to stronger customer relationships and increased sales.

See also:

Marketing Fundamentals: Marketing Ethics

Chapter 30

Pareto's Principle

The 80/20 rule, also known as the Pareto principle, is a concept that explains how 80% of the outcomes or results come from 20% of the inputs or causes. The principle was first introduced by Italian economist Vilfredo Pareto, who observed that 80% of the wealth in Italy was owned by 20% of the population. This concept has been applied to various fields, including business, where it is commonly used to optimise operations, maximise efficiency, and improve decision-making.

The Pareto Principle Applied to Business

The 80/20 rule is widely used in business to analyse customer behaviours, sales, and revenue. It is a powerful tool that helps businesses identify the most profitable customers, products, and services and allocate resources accordingly. Here are examples of how the 80/20 rule applies in business.

Customer Behaviour: As a general rule of thumb, 20% of the customers account for 80% of the revenue. These customers are often the most loyal and profitable, and it's in any business's interest to identify and cater to their needs. By understanding buying patterns, preferences, and behaviour, businesses can develop targeted marketing campaigns, create personalised experiences, and increase customer retention.

Sales: The 80/20 rule also applies to sales. In most businesses, 20% of the sales team generates 80% of the revenue. These top performers are usually the most experienced, knowledgeable, and skilled salespeople, and they are critical to success. By identifying these top performers, businesses can provide the necessary support, training, and resources to maximise their potential and replicate their success across the sales team.

Revenue: The 80/20 rule also applies to revenue. In most businesses, 80% of the revenue comes from 20% of the products or services. These high-margin products or services are the most profitable, and businesses must focus on them to generate maximum revenue. By analysing sales data and customer behaviours, businesses can identify these products or services and allocate resources accordingly, such as investing in marketing, improving quality, or expanding the product line.

The 80/20 rule has many benefits for businesses, including:

- **Optimising resources:** By focusing on the most profitable customers, products, and services, businesses can allocate resources more efficiently and effectively.

- **Improving decision-making:** The 80/20 rule provides valuable insights into customer behaviours, sales, and revenue, which can help businesses make informed decisions and prioritise initiatives.

- **Increasing profitability:** By focusing on the most profitable customers, products, and services, businesses can increase profitability and achieve long-term success.

Limitations of the Pareto Principle

However, the 80/20 rule also has its limitations. Some potential drawbacks are:

- **Oversimplification:** The 80/20 rule is generalised and may only apply to some businesses or situations. Depending on their industry, size, and other factors, some businesses may have different ratios, such as 90/10 or 70/30.

- **Limited perspective:** The 80/20 rule only focuses on a small portion of the business, such as the most profitable customers, products, or services. This narrow perspective may overlook other important factors, such as customer satisfaction, brand reputation, or employee engagement.

Businesses should focus their efforts and resources on the areas most likely to generate the highest returns.

See also:

Market Analysis: The SWOT Framework
Market Analysis: Bowman's Strategic Clock
Market Analysis: Competition
Marketing Mix: Price
Marketing Mix: Place
Marketing Measurement: Data Analysis

VI

Marketing
Communication

Chapter 31

Marketing & Advertising

Advertising is often the most visible aspect of marketing. It is the part that people encounter regularly through various media channels, such as television, billboards, and online ads. Since advertising is easily noticeable and can have a significant impact, it overshadows other marketing components. As a result, people may mistakenly assume that advertising represents the entirety of marketing. This playbook aims to address this confusion by emphasising the comprehensive nature of marketing, highlighting its various components beyond advertising.

There is no denying, however, that historically advertising has been an integral part of marketing efforts. Before the advent of digital marketing and the diversification of marketing channels, traditional advertising methods like print, radio, and television played a dominant role. Nowadays, media outlets, in their coverage and discussions, often focus on advertising due to its widespread appeal and impact. This section will explore the differences between marketing and advertising, while the following chapters will each focus on a particular communication channel and the best way to run effective campaigns.

Marketing

Marketing is a broader concept than advertising, encompassing all the activities involved in identifying and satisfying customer needs through product development, pricing, promotion, and distribution. Marketing is a process that begins with market research to identify consumer needs and preferences; is followed by product development to create products that meet those needs; and finally, culminates with promotion and distribution to make those products available to consumers.

For example, a company that produces health supplements may conduct market research to identify the nutritional needs of their target audience, develop new supplements that meet those needs, price the products competitively, promote the supplements through advertising and public relations, and distribute them online and offline channels.

Advertising

Advertising is a specific subset of marketing that focuses on promoting a product or service through paid communication channels, such as television, radio, print, or digital media. It aims to create awareness, interest, and desire for a product or service and to persuade consumers to take a specific action, such as making a purchase or visiting a website.

Advertising activities include creating and placing advertisements in various media channels, such as television, radio, print, or online. Advertising aims to reach the target audience with a compelling message that resonates with their needs and desires and encourages them to take action.

For example, a company that sells sports equipment may run a television advertisement during a major sporting event, highlighting the benefits of its products and encouraging viewers to visit its website or store to purchase the equipment.

Differences between Marketing and Advertising

Scope

The scope of marketing is much broader than advertising, encompassing all the activities involved in identifying and satisfying customer needs. Marketing involves everything from market research and product development to pricing, promotion, and distribution. Advertising is a subset of marketing focusing on promoting a product or service through paid communication channels.

Purpose

Marketing aims to identify customer needs, create products that meet those needs and promote and distribute those products to the target audience. It aims to build long-term customer relationships by satisfying their needs and creating value. The purpose of advertising is to create awareness, interest, and desire for a product or service and to persuade consumers to take a specific action, such as making a purchase or visiting a website.

Methods

Marketing activities involve various methods, such as market research, product development, pricing, promotion, and distribution. These methods are designed to identify customer needs, create products that meet those needs, and promote and distribute those products to the target audience. Advertising involves creating and placing advertisements in various media channels, such as television, radio, print, or online.

To illustrate the differences between marketing and advertising, let's look at some examples.

Example 1: Apple

Apple is a company known for its innovative products and marketing strategies. The company uses a range of marketing activities to identify and satisfy customer needs, including market research, product development, pricing, promotion, and distribution. For example, Apple may conduct market research to identify customer needs and preferences, develop new products that meet those needs, price them competitively, promote them through advertising and public relations, and distribute them online and offline channels.

Advertising is also an essential part of Apple's marketing strategy, but it is just one component. Apple's advertisements focus on creating a desire for their products, often emphasising their innovative design and user experience. For example, Apple's 'Think Different' campaign positioned Apple as a brand that challenges the status quo.

Example 2: Coca-Cola

Coca-Cola is a global brand that uses marketing and advertising to promote its products to consumers worldwide. Coca-Cola's marketing activities include market research, product development, pricing, promotion, and distribution. For example, Coca-Cola may conduct market research to understand consumer preferences in different regions, develop new flavours and packaging to appeal to local tastes, price their products competitively, promote their products through advertising and sponsorships, and distribute their products through a range of channels, from supermarkets to vending machines.

Coca-Cola's advertising campaigns are known for their creativity and emotional appeal. The company's 'Share a Coke' campaign, which began in Australia in 2011 and has since been rolled out globally, encouraged consumers to personalise Coca-Cola bottles with their names or the names of loved ones. The campaign was hugely successful, generating a 2.5% increase in sales and reaching more than 70 countries. Coca-Cola's advertising also emphasises the brand's association with happiness, sharing, and togetherness, often featuring feel-good music and images of people enjoying life.

Why Businesses Advertise

Advertising is a critical component of any successful business strategy. It helps businesses communicate their products and services to potential customers and build brand awareness. Effective advertising can attract new customers, increase sales, and build brand loyalty. Here are some key reasons why advertising is important for businesses:

- **Attracting new customers:** Advertising is a powerful tool for reaching new customers and increasing sales. Using a combination of media channels, businesses can target specific demographics and reach potential customers who may not be aware of their products or services. This can help businesses increase their customer base and expand their reach.

- **Building brand awareness:** Advertising effectively builds brand awareness and creates a strong brand identity. By using consistent branding and messaging across different channels, businesses can create a sense of familiarity and trust with their target audience. This can help businesses stand out in a crowded marketplace and establish themselves as a credible and trustworthy brand.

- **Communicating value:** Advertising can help businesses communicate the value of their products and services to potential customers. By highlighting their products' benefits and unique features, businesses can demonstrate why they are superior to their competitors. This can help businesses differentiate themselves in a competitive market and attract customers looking for high-quality products or services.

- **Creating customer loyalty:** Advertising can help businesses build long-term relationships by creating a sense of loyalty and trust. By using consistent messaging and branding, businesses can create a positive association with their brand and products in the minds of their customers. This can lead to repeat business and customer referrals, critical for sustained growth.

- **Staying competitive:** Advertising is essential for businesses that want to stay competitive in a constantly evolving marketplace. By keeping their products and services top of mind with their target audience, businesses can maintain their market share and grow. Advertising can also help businesses adapt to changing consumer trends and preferences, which is critical for staying relevant and competitive.

Misconceptions about Advertising

While advertising is often exposed to much scrutiny by the public, there is a limited understanding of its scope and many misconceptions about how it influences purchase decisions. Let's address some of the most common ones.

- **Advertising guarantees immediate success:** One of the most prevalent misconceptions is that advertising alone can instantly generate substantial sales and success for a business. While advertising is a powerful tool for reaching target audiences and promoting products or services, its impact is often cumulative and requires consistent effort over time. Building brand awareness, establishing trust, and influencing consumer behaviours usually takes time and a well-executed strategy.

- **All advertising is manipulative:** There is a misconception that all advertising is inherently manipulative and designed to deceive consumers into buying products they don't need. While unethical advertising practices have existed, most advertising focuses on informing, persuading, and creating awareness about products or services that genuinely add value to consumers' lives. Effective advertising relies on building trust and maintaining transparent communication with consumers.

- **Advertising is only about creativity and entertainment:** Many people believe that advertising is solely about creating catchy slogans, entertaining commercials, and memorable jingles. While creativity plays a crucial role in advertising, successful campaigns also require strategic thinking, market research, data analysis, and a deep understanding of the target audience. Effective advertising aligns creativity with business objectives and consumer preferences.

- **Any publicity is good publicity:** This misconception suggests that any type of attention, even negative publicity, benefits a brand or product. While controversial or attention-grabbing campaigns can generate buzz, they can damage a brand's reputation and alienate consumers. Positive brand perception, ethical practices, and aligning advertising messages with consumer values are vital for long-term success.

- **Advertising is only for large businesses with big budgets:** Another common misconception is that advertising is exclusively reserved for large corporations with substantial budgets. While big brands may have larger advertising budgets, businesses of all sizes can benefit from tailored and cost-effective advertising strategies. The digital age has opened numerous affordable advertising channels, such as social media, influencer partnerships, and targeted online advertising, allowing smaller businesses to compete effectively.

Marketing and advertising are not the same.

See also:

Marketing Fundamentals: What is Marketing
The Marketing Mix: Promotion

Chapter 32

Copywriting

Copywriting is one of the most important aspects of marketing. It involves the creation of written content for advertising, marketing, and other promotional efforts and can come in various forms, including website copy, blog posts, and social media updates, to name a few. Well-written copy in marketing aims to capture the reader's attention, engage them, and ultimately persuade them to take action, whether buying a product, subscribing to a service, or signing up for a newsletter. In this chapter, we will explore the importance of copywriting, what good copywriting looks like in advertising, and provide tips on improving a business's copywriting skills.

The Importance of Copywriting in Marketing

Copywriting is critical to the success of any marketing campaign. The quality of the copy can determine whether a potential customer is interested in a product or service. Good copywriting can make a product or service stand out from the competition, increase engagement with a target audience, and ultimately drive sales.

From a technical point of view, copywriting can also improve search engine optimisation (SEO) by including relevant keywords and phrases. This helps improve the ranking of a website in search engine results pages, making it easier for potential customers to find the website.

What Good Copywriting Looks Like in Advertising

Effective copywriting can make the difference between a successful and a failed campaign. Most importantly, good copywriting is not just writing. It's also: research, storytelling, images, graphics, editing, rewriting, and applied psychology. The following factors are important to keep in mind:

- **Clear and concise:** Good copywriting is easy to understand and gets straight to the point. It should be written in simple language that is easily digestible by the target audience.

- **Engaging:** Quality copy captures the reader's attention and keeps them engaged. It should be written in an interesting, informative, and entertaining way.

- **Persuasive:** Ultimately, copywriting in marketing should persuade the reader to take action. This can be done through strong, persuasive language and compelling calls to action.

- **Relevant:** To drive action, the copy should be relevant to the target audience by addressing their needs, concerns, and interests.

- **Unique:** Good copywriting stands out from the competition. It should be unique and memorable, leaving a lasting impression on the reader.

Examples of Good Copywriting

Writing strong copy is becoming increasingly important in consumer communications, specifically advertising. Here are some brilliant examples of copywriting that drove effective communication and, as a result, business results in the long term.

- **'Got Milk'?** - This campaign was created by the advertising agency Goodby Silverstein & Partners in the 1990s to promote milk consumption. The campaign featured a series of TV ads and print ads that used witty and humorous copywriting to emphasise the importance of having milk on hand. One of the most memorable ads featured a man trying to answer a radio contest question with a mouth full of peanut butter and no milk to wash it down. The tagline 'Got Milk'? became a pop culture phenomenon and is still remembered today.

- **'Think Different'** - This was an advertising campaign created by Apple in 1997 to promote its brand and products. The campaign featured a series of TV and print ads celebrating iconic figures throughout history known for their creativity, innovation, and non-conformity. The copywriting used in the ads was simple but powerful, with the tagline 'Think Different' encapsulating Apple's brand philosophy and positioning the company as a leader in creativity and innovation.

- **'Just Do It'** - This tagline was created by the advertising agency Wieden+Kennedy for Nike in 1988. The campaign featured a series of TV and print ads that celebrated the spirit of athleticism and encouraged people to push their limits and overcome obstacles. The copywriting used in the ads was bold and inspiring. The tagline, 'Just Do It', became a cultural catchphrase that encapsulated Nike's brand values and has been used across all their ads and marketing campaigns since its inception.

Tips for Improving Copywriting Skills

Copywriting is a learned skill that takes practice and patience, but it is a key skill for every marketer to master. Even if the role does not include writing copy, it's still essential to understand how good copy should be evaluated as part of the marketing campaign process.

- **Know The Audience:** Understanding the target audience is essential to effective copywriting. This includes their demographics, interests, and pain points. Knowing this information can help tailor the message to resonate better with the audience.

- **Keep it Simple:** Good copywriting is easy to understand. Avoid using complicated language or industry jargon that may confuse the audience.

- **Write with Purpose:** Every copy should have a clear purpose. Whether to inform, persuade, or entertain, ensure the copy serves its intended purpose.

- **Use Powerful Words:** The right words can be compelling in copywriting. Use words that evoke emotion and create a sense of urgency, such as 'limited-time offer' or 'exclusive'.

- **Focus on Benefits:** Instead of focusing on the features of a product or service, focus on the benefits. How will it improve the customer's life? What problems will it solve? This can be much more effective in persuading customers to take action.

- **Use Social Proof:** Social proof can be a powerful tool in copywriting. Including customer testimonials, reviews, or endorsements can help build trust and credibility with potential customers.

- **Edit Ruthlessly:** Good copywriting requires careful editing. Eliminate any unnecessary words or phrases and make sure the copy flows smoothly.

Good copywriting is clear, engaging, persuasive, relevant, and unique.

See also:

Consumer Behaviour: Social Proof
Marketing Communication: Search Engine Optimisation

Chapter 33

Advertising Types By Objective

Advertising is an important tool for businesses to promote their products and services. However, not all types of advertising are effective for all types of business objectives. In this chapter, we will discuss the different types of advertising that businesses can use based on the AIDA model.

The AIDA Model

The AIDA model is the most used tool to codify consumers moving through the decision tree to buy a product . It was initially introduced by American Advertising Advocate Elias St. Elmo Lewisin in 1903 and is one of the longest-serving marketing models. The AIDA model describes a funnel that moves from Awareness → Interest → Desire → Action. It's a hierarchical and linear model that implies consumers walk through several steps to purchase.

The steps proposed by the AIDA model are as follows:

Attention – The consumer becomes aware of a category, product, or brand (usually through advertising)

Interest – The consumer becomes interested in learning about brand benefits, and how the brand fits with lifestyle.

Desire – The consumer develops a favourable disposition towards the brand

Action – The consumer forms a purchase intention, shops around, engages in a trial, or makes a purchase

The Marketing Funnel Strategy

The overarching strategy behind the marketing funnel is that marketers should guide as many consumers through the stages of awareness until action as possible, using various efforts.

- **The attention stage** - During this stage, a marketer's primary objective is to capture their audience's attention to make them aware of the brand and the products they sell. Marketers must understand their target audience and make target customers aware of their brand through various communications tools such as advertising, social media, direct marketing, search engine optimisation (SEO), or others.

- **The interest stage** - How can marketers reinforce interest in a product? The marketer must reiterate how the brand or product can solve the customer's problem. It is also vital that the company provides customers with all the information they are looking for. For example, email campaigns, webinars, blogs, etc., can be effective methods. This way, the marketer can start nurturing the relationship with leads, and cultivate the beginning of a potential long-term customer relationship.

- **The desire stage** - Desire tends to be the longest stage of the marketing funnel. During this stage, marketers should help customers decide to purchase the product. Some methods include maintaining customer communication, answering questions or queries, or presenting them with reliable reviews.

- **The action stage** - This stage is the final step of the funnel, where customers have decided to purchase the product. Marketers' main goal is to convince customers to buy as soon as possible. Through promotions, exclusive discounts, bundles, etc. Marketers must also ensure the brand leaves a positive impression on the customer.

Following this model, we define four different types of advertising, which also leads to a further classification of advertising channels. Certain channels, such as social media advertising, lend themselves naturally to one or the other part of the four-stage process.

Attention-based Advertising

The first step is to get the audience's attention. Attention-based advertising creates awareness and generates interest in a product or service. The goal is to make the audience aware of the product or service and spark their interest.

- **Billboards** are large outdoor advertising structures on busy highways and roads. They are designed to catch the attention of drivers and passengers and convey a brand's message quickly.

- **Social Media Ads** on platforms like Facebook, Twitter, Instagram, and TikTok offer various ad formats designed to grab users' attention as they scroll through their feeds. These ads can be images, videos, or carousel ads that allow users to swipe through multiple images.

- **Display Ads** are digital ads on websites designed to grab users' attention as they browse the internet. They can be banners, pop-ups, or video ads that play before or during online content.

- **Guerrilla Marketing** is a non-traditional advertising technique that uses unconventional tactics to create buzz and generate attention. Examples of guerrilla marketing include flash mobs, street art, and viral campaigns.

- **Sponsorship** is a form of advertising where a company pays to be associated with a particular event, sports team, or celebrity. This can be an effective way to generate attention and build brand awareness.

- **Product Placement** is where a brand pays to have its product featured in a TV show, movie, or other form of entertainment. This can effectively get a product in front of a large audience and generate attention.

- **In-Game Advertising** involves placing ads within video games. This can be sponsored content, product placement, or even in-game billboards. As gaming becomes more popular, in-game advertising is becoming an increasingly effective way to capture the attention of younger audiences.

Interest-based Advertising

Once the audience's attention is captured, the next step is to keep their interest. Interest-based advertising is designed to provide more information about the product or service and to create a desire for it.

- **Social Media Advertising** can also target specific demographics and interests, allowing businesses to reach their ideal audience. Examples include sponsored posts on Facebook or Instagram, promoted tweets on Twitter, and sponsored content on LinkedIn.

- **Content Marketing** creates and shares valuable content to attract and engage a target audience. By providing valuable information or entertainment to potential customers, businesses can build trust and establish themselves as thought leaders in their industry. Examples of content marketing include blog posts, videos, podcasts, and e-books.

Desire-Based Advertising

After generating interest, the goal is to create a desire for the product or service. Desire-based advertising is designed to connect emotionally with the audience and make them want the product or service.

- **Search Engine Marketing** (SEM) involves placing ads on search engine results pages (SERPs). When someone searches for a keyword related to the business, the ad will appear at the top of the search results. This type of advertising is particularly effective for businesses with a strong online presence. Examples of SEM include Google Ads and Bing Ads.

- **Display Advertising** is the term coined for placing ads on third-party websites. These ads can target specific demographics or interests, allowing businesses to reach their ideal audience. Display advertising includes banner ads, pop-up ads, and native ads.

- **Influencer Marketing,** as it says in the name, is all about partnering with influential people on social media to promote a product or service. This type of advertising can be particularly effective for reaching younger audiences, who often trust the opinions of social media influencers more than traditional advertising. Examples of influencer marketing include sponsored Instagram posts or YouTube videos.

- **Retargeting** is showing ads to people who have interacted with the business. For example, if someone visits the website but doesn't make a purchase, a business can show them ads for the product they are interested in on other websites they visit. This type of advertising can be particularly effective for driving conversions.

Action-Based Advertising

Finally, advertising aims to get the audience to act, such as purchasing or signing up for a service. Action-based advertising is designed to provide a clear call to action and make it easy for the audience to take the desired action.

- **Direct Mail Advertising** involves sending physical mail to potential customers. While this type of advertising can be expensive, it can also be highly targeted and effective. Examples of direct mail advertising include postcards, catalogues, and letters.

- **Email Marketing** means sending promotional emails to people who have opted-in to receive them. This type of advertising can be highly effective for driving sales and building customer loyalty. Email marketing includes newsletters, promotional emails, and abandoned cart emails.

- **In-Store Advertising** is the term used for placing ads or promotional materials in a physical store. This type of advertising can be highly effective for driving in-store purchases. Examples of in-store advertising include product displays, shelf talkers, and floor graphics.

The choice of advertising channels for a campaign should be objective and audience led.

See also:

Marketing Communication: TV Advertising
Marketing Communication: Print Advertising
Marketing Communication: Radio Advertising
Marketing Communication: Out-of-Home Advertising
Marketing Communication: Public Relations
Marketing Communication: Word-of-Mouth Advertising
Marketing Communication: Influencer Marketing

Chapter 34

TV Advertising

TV advertising remains important due to its extensive reach and ability to engage viewers. Television has a massive audience, allowing brands to target diverse demographics. It enables companies to simultaneously showcase their products or services to millions of viewers, maximising brand exposure and market penetration. TV advertising also possesses a persuasive impact, utilising visuals, music, and narrative techniques to create emotional connections and influence consumer behaviour.

TV advertising has faced speculation about its decline in the face of digital media advancements. However, it is essential to recognise that TV advertising is far from dead. In fact, it continues to hold significant value and relevance in today's marketing landscape, especially when combined with digital presence. According to eMarketer, TV ad spending in the United States is projected to reach $70.30 billion in 2023, indicating that advertisers still value investing in TV commercials. In addition, according to Nielsen's Total Audience Report, 87% of US adults aged 18 and older watch traditional TV weekly. Across the pond, a similar picture emerges. In the UK, the average daily TV viewing time per individual in 2021 was 3 hours and 22 minutes, according to BARB (Broadcasters' Audience Research Board), and TV advertising accounted for 23.3% of total ad spend in 2020, according to the Advertising Association/WARC Expenditure Report. Looking further east, TV advertising remains strong in Asian markets. In India, for example, TV is the dominant advertising medium, with a significant share of ad spend. According to the Indian Broadcasting Foundation, TV advertising accounted for 37% of total advertising expenditure in 2020, and according to Video Research Ltd., the average daily TV viewing time per household in Japan was 3 hours and 44 minutes in the same year.

Benefits of TV

TV has become a powerful tool in a larger toolbox that marketers use nowadays to drive awareness and consumer engagement. TV, in particular, excels at the following factors:

- **Massive Reach:** TV advertising remains unrivalled in its ability to reach a vast and diverse audience. Despite the proliferation of digital platforms, television continues to be a primary source of entertainment and information for millions of people. It provides an unparalleled opportunity to connect with various demographics simultaneously, ensuring broad exposure for brands and their messages.

- **Engaging and Impactful:** TV ads possess a unique power to captivate and engage viewers. Combining sight, sound, and motion creates a compelling and immersive experience. Well-crafted TV commercials can evoke emotions, tell compelling stories, and leave a lasting impact on audiences. Other advertising mediums cannot easily replicate this level of engagement.

- **Brand Building and Trust:** TV advertising is crucial in brand building. By leveraging the power of television, companies can create strong brand identities and establish themselves as reputable and trustworthy entities. TV ads' visual and auditory elements build familiarity, recognition, and emotional connections with consumers, fostering long-term brand loyalty.

- **Complementary to Digital Channels:** Rather than being replaced by digital advertising, TV advertising synergises with online marketing efforts. It serves as a complementary component of an integrated marketing strategy. TV ads can create awareness and generate brand interest, which can be further explored through digital channels. TV advertising drives online searches, website visits, social media engagement, and other digital interactions.

- **Event-based and Shared Experience:** Television continues to be a platform for shared experiences, especially during major events such as sports championships, award shows, or cultural phenomena. These moments unite people, creating opportunities for advertisers to connect with audiences on a large scale. TV ads aired during these events can generate buzz, spark conversations, and extend their reach through social media and other online platforms.

- **Targeted Advertising Advances:** While TV advertising was traditionally perceived as lacking in targeting capabilities, technology has evolved to enhance its precision. Advanced audience measurement tools, programmatic ad buying, and addressable TV advertising have enabled more targeted and personalised approaches. Advertisers can now deliver tailored messages to specific audience segments, optimizing their reach and impact.

Types of TV Advertising

When companies are deciding between different types of TV advertising, it's important to consider their marketing goals, target audience, budget, and the specific message they want to convey.

- **Broadcast TV Advertising:** Broadcast TV advertising involves airing commercials during scheduled programs on widely available television channels. It offers a broad reach, allowing companies to target various viewers. For example, ABC Electronics wants to promote its new line of smartphones to a large audience. They air their commercials during prime time slots on popular channels, ensuring their message reaches a wide demographic.

- **Cable TV Advertising:** Cable TV advertising involves commercials on specific cable television networks. It offers a more targeted approach than broadcast TV, allowing companies to reach specific audiences based on the network's programming. For instance, a fitness equipment company named FitZone wants to target health-conscious individuals. They air their commercial on a cable network that primarily broadcasts fitness and wellness-related shows, ensuring that their message reaches their desired audience.

- **Spot TV Advertising:** Spot TV advertising involves airing commercials in specific local markets or regions. It allows companies to target specific geographical areas where their target audience is concentrated. For example, a local restaurant called Gourmet Delights wants to attract customers in a particular city. They decide to air their commercial on local TV stations within that city, ensuring their message reaches potential customers.

- **Sponsorship Advertising:** Sponsorship advertising involves associating a company's brand with a specific TV program, event, or sports team. It allows companies to brand recognition and create positive associations with sponsored content. For instance, a sports apparel company called ActiveSport sponsors a popular football league. By displaying its brand logo during the games and featuring its products in related promotional materials, ActiveSport increases brand visibility and establishes a strong connection with football fans.

- **Product Placement:** Product placement involves featuring a company's product or brand in TV shows or movies. It allows companies to integrate their offerings seamlessly into the storyline, gaining exposure and influencing viewers in a non-disruptive manner. For example, a beverage company named CoolFizz strikes a product placement deal with a popular TV drama series. The characters are frequently seen drinking CoolFizz beverages, creating subconscious associations between the brand and enjoyable moments for the viewers.

TV Commercial Story Structure

The structure of a TV commercial is of paramount importance, as it directly influences its effectiveness in capturing and retaining viewer attention. A well-structured commercial follows a clear narrative arc, starting with a compelling opening that grabs the audience's interest, leading to a concise and impactful message, and concluding with a strong call to action.

By crafting a coherent and engaging structure, advertisers maximise the commercial's impact, enhance brand recognition, and increase the likelihood of achieving their desired marketing objectives. In general, we can identify 6 common types of structures:

Extremise the benefit - Here, the advert focuses on the product's benefit. The result is often heavily extremised, often displaying an out-of-this-world payoff. An example could be a diet yoghurt that tastes so light and fresh that the person eating it takes off and lands on a cloud showing enjoyment of the delicious taste of the product. The plot may emphasize the low-calorie or low-fat nature of the yoghurt, highlighting its suitability for those seeking a healthier lifestyle. Additionally, the advert may incorporate visually appealing product shots, showcasing its creamy texture and vibrant flavours.

Extremise the need - This copy focuses on moments or needs where the product or service is necessary. A great example is the Snickers 'You're Not You When You're Hungry' advert, which revolves around a humorous and exaggerated portrayal of how people's personalities change when they are hungry. The advert typically features a scenario where an individual acts out of character, displays strange behaviour or struggles to perform everyday tasks. This behaviour is then contrasted with the transformative power of eating a Snickers bar, which instantly restores the person to their normal self. The plot emphasizes that hunger can negatively impact one's mood and capabilities, but Snickers can quickly satisfy hunger and bring back the person's true self, highlighting the brand's ability to provide a satisfying and energizing snack.

Analogy - An analogy is a literary device that compares two different things or concepts to highlight their similarities or make a complex idea easier to understand. It involves drawing parallels between unrelated subjects based on shared characteristics, functions, or relationships. Evian put this concept into practice as part of their baby advert. The main plot of the Evian baby advert centres around a whimsical and imaginative concept that features adults encountering their baby selves reflected in mirrors or windows. As the adults notice their infantile reflections, they are compelled to engage in joyful and playful movements. The advert showcases babies' carefree and uninhibited nature, contrasting it with adults' more serious and restrained behaviour. The iconic Evian brand logo is integrated into the scenes, reinforcing that drinking Evian water helps individuals reconnect with their youthful and vibrant selves. The plot aims to evoke a sense of nostalgia, innocence, and joy while promoting the brand's message of purity and vitality.

Endorsement - This type of advert usually features a person of status or celebrity known for a particular preference, skill or feature. A common product category that uses endorsements for its adverts is toothbrush or toothpaste brands. The advert often begins with a scene at a dental clinic, where a dentist discusses the importance of oral hygiene and the role of a good toothbrush in maintaining a healthy smile. The dentist then highlights the features and benefits of Oral-B toothbrushes, such as superior plaque removal, gentle bristles, and advanced technology for optimal oral care. The plot may also include testimonials from patients who have experienced positive results after using Oral-B products. The advert aims to build credibility and reassure viewers that Oral-B is a reliable choice for oral care needs by featuring a trusted dental expert.

Problem > Solution - One of the most common structures follows the simple problem-solution framework. A general story structure would be as follows. The advert presents a relatable problem that viewers can identify, capturing their frustration or inconvenience. It then introduces the advertised product or service as the solution, showcasing its features, benefits, and unique selling points. The advert demonstrates how the solution effortlessly resolves the problem through engaging visuals, testimonials, and before-and-after scenarios. With an optimistic and uplifting tone, it connects with viewers emotionally and encourages them to take action. By the end, viewers are left with a clear understanding of the problem, the solution, and its positive impact on their lives, driving them to seek more information or purchase.

Proof of delivering the benefit - Also called RTB (reason to believe) copy, this often features direct product comparison in the advert. Categories commonly making use of this are hygiene products or detergent adverts. The advert visually compares the two pads, emphasizing their key features and benefits. It may showcase absorption, comfort, leak protection, or flexibility. The plot often includes scenes or testimonials from women who have experienced the advantages of the featured pad, highlighting their satisfaction and confidence in using it. The advert aims to empower women by showcasing a pad that provides optimal protection, comfort, and reliability, ultimately encouraging viewers to choose the advertised pad as their preferred choice for feminine hygiene.

TV maintains its mass reach qualities and is a powerful story telling platform.

See also:

Marketing Fundamentals: Marketing Budget
Market Analysis: Consumer Profiling
Market Analysis: Insights
Brand Building: Brand Positioning
Marketing Communication: Copywriting
Marketing Measurement: Data Analysis
Marketing Measurement: Key Performance Indicators

Chapter 35

Print Advertising

Print advertising has long been a prominent and effective marketing tool for businesses, offering a tangible and visually engaging medium to reach target audiences. This chapter provides an in-depth overview of print advertising, exploring its effectiveness and various forms, and guiding businesses in choosing the appropriate approach based on their campaign objectives.

The History of Print Advertising

The history of print advertising traces back centuries, with the development of printing technology playing a significant role in its evolution. From humble beginnings to the modern era, print advertising has transformed how businesses promote their products and services to consumers.

- **Early Origins:** The origins of print advertising can be traced back to ancient civilisations, where simple advertisements were etched onto walls or written on papyrus. These early advertisements served to announce events and sales or promote goods and services.

- **The Gutenberg Revolution:** The invention of the printing press by Johannes Gutenberg in the 15th century revolutionised the field of printing and marked a significant milestone in the history of print advertising. This invention enabled the mass production of printed materials, including books, pamphlets, and newspapers, laying the foundation for disseminating advertisements on a larger scale.

- **Emergence of Newspapers and Magazines:** The 17th and 18th centuries witnessed the rise of newspapers and magazines that provided a platform for advertisements to reach wider audiences. As literacy rates increased, newspapers became popular mediums for advertising, featuring classified ads, announcements, and promotional messages. Through their specialised content and niche readerships, magazines offered targeted advertising opportunities for businesses catering to specific interests or demographics.

- **Industrialization and the Birth of Brands:** With the advent of the Industrial Revolution in the 19th century, mass production and consumerism surged. This era marked the birth of well-known brands and the need for companies to differentiate themselves through advertising. Print advertisements began to adopt more elaborate designs and persuasive techniques to capture consumer attention and build brand recognition.

- **Rise of Advertising Agencies:** In the late 19th and early 20th centuries, advertising agencies emerged to meet the growing demand for professional advertising services. These agencies specialise in creating and placing print advertisements on behalf of businesses. Their expertise in market research, copywriting, and design contributed to the development of more sophisticated and effective print campaigns.

- **Technological Advancements:** The 20th century witnessed significant technological advancements that influenced the landscape of print advertising. Introducing offset printing, colour printing, and photographic techniques allowed for more visually appealing and impactful advertisements. As radio and television gained prominence, print advertising adapted and integrated with these new media platforms.

- **Digital Revolution and Print Advertising:** The digital revolution of the late 20th century and the rise of the internet brought about profound changes in the advertising industry. Digital advertising channels, such as online banners and social media platforms, gained popularity, leading to speculation about the decline of print advertising. However, print advertising has maintained relevance by offering tangible and targeted marketing opportunities that complement digital strategies.

Effectiveness of Print Advertising

Print advertising continues to be a powerful communication tool, offering several compelling reasons for its effectiveness.

- **Credibility and Trust:** Print ads are often perceived as more trustworthy than digital advertisements, as they are physically present and can be easily verified. The tangible nature of print media instils a sense of credibility among consumers, enhancing their trust in the advertised message.

- **Targeted Reach:** Print media allows businesses to target specific geographic regions, demographics, or niche audiences effectively. By selecting the appropriate print publications, businesses can ensure their messages reach the right readers, increasing the likelihood of generating leads and conversions.

- **Engagement and Attention:** Print ads demand the reader's attention due to their physical presence. Print media provides a focused and immersive experience with fewer distractions and no click-away options, enabling advertisers to convey their message effectively. Additionally, readers often spend more time engaging with print materials, allowing deeper brand exposure.

- **Brand Recognition and Longevity:** Print ads can create lasting brand recognition using consistent visual branding elements. Newspapers, magazines, billboards, and brochures can be tangible reminders, reinforcing brand associations over time. This longevity can contribute to customer loyalty and repeat business.

Types of Print Advertising

Print advertising encompasses various formats, offering unique advantages and targeting different audience segments. Understanding the available options helps businesses tailor their advertising strategies accordingly.

- **Newspapers:** Newspapers are a traditional and widely circulated form of print media. They offer a diverse readership and allow businesses to reach a broad audience or target specific regions. Local newspapers are particularly effective for geographically targeted campaigns, while national or international publications cater to broader demographics.

- **Magazines:** Magazines are niche-oriented publications that cater to specific interests or demographics. Businesses can choose magazines that align with their target audience's preferences, ensuring their print ads reach a highly engaged readership. Magazines often offer specialized content, such as lifestyle, fashion, or industry-specific topics.

- **Trade Publications:** Trade publications are industry-specific magazines or journals. They focus on a particular sector or profession, allowing businesses to directly target professionals within a specific field. Advertising in trade publications ensures messages reach a concentrated audience interested in industry-related news, products, and services.

- **Consumer and Lifestyle Publications:** Consumer and lifestyle publications cover various topics, including travel, health, home, and entertainment. These publications attract readers with specific interests, providing businesses with opportunities to showcase products or services relevant to their target audience's lifestyles.

- **Brochures and Catalogues:** Brochures and catalogues serve as standalone advertising materials that can be distributed in various locations or sent directly to potential customers. They offer a comprehensive and detailed representation of a business's offerings, making them suitable for industries requiring in-depth information or showcasing a wide range of products.

How to Choose Publications for Print Advertising

- **Target Audience:** Understanding the target audience's demographics, interests, and behaviours is crucial. Businesses should select publications that align with their target market's characteristics to ensure their print ads resonate with the intended readership.

- **Circulation and Readership:** Evaluating a publication's circulation figures and readership demographics helps businesses gauge their print ads' reach and potential impact. Analysing data on audience size, geographic distribution, and reader profiles aids in determining which publications are most likely to engage the desired target audience.

- **Editorial Alignment:** Considering a publication's editorial content and focus is essential. Businesses should ensure their print ads align with the publication's tone, values, and target readership. An advertisement seamlessly integrating with the overall content enhances its effectiveness and increases its chances of capturing readers' attention.

- **Advertising Costs:** Businesses must assess their budget and compare advertising costs in different publications. While more prominent publications may have higher advertising rates, they often offer wider reach and better visibility. Smaller or more niche publications may provide more targeted exposure at a lower cost.

- **Competitor Analysis:** Analysing competitors' advertising strategies within a specific industry can offer insights into successful placement opportunities. Businesses should identify the publications where competitors are advertising and assess the impact and relevance of those platforms to inform their own advertising decisions.

Elements of a Successful Print Advert

- **Compelling Visual Design:** A visually appealing and well-designed print advert immediately grabs attention. Businesses should consider using high-quality images, vibrant colours, and clear typography to create an eye-catching layout that effectively communicates the intended message.

- **Concise and Persuasive Copy:** Print adverts should feature concise and persuasive copy that conveys the key message quickly. Captivating headlines, clear product descriptions, and compelling calls to action engage readers and prompt them to act. Businesses should focus on crafting copy that highlights the unique selling points of their products or services and addresses the needs and desires of the target audience.

- **Clear Branding:** A good print advert incorporates strong branding elements to ensure immediate recognition and association with the business. This includes featuring the company logo, using consistent brand colours and fonts, and maintaining a cohesive visual identity throughout the advert.

- **Relevant and Memorable Content:** Print adverts should deliver content that resonates with the target audience and creates a memorable impression. This can be achieved through storytelling, humour, emotional appeal, or unique creative approaches that make the advert stand out from competitors.

- **Call-to-Action:** A clear and compelling call-to-action is essential to prompt readers to take the desired action. Whether visiting a website, purchasing, or contacting the business, a strong call-to-action guides readers towards the next step and facilitates conversion.

- **Ad Placement:** The placement of the advert within the publication is crucial for its effectiveness. Businesses should consider page position, relevance to relevant content, and prominence to maximize visibility and engagement.

Example of a Successful Print Ad

Apple, a renowned technology company, created an impactful print advert with the iconic tagline 'Think Different', which revolutionised how technology was perceived and positioned Apple as an innovative and visionary brand.

- **Bold and Minimalistic Design:** The print advert employed a bold and minimalistic design approach that immediately captured attention. Against a clean white background, the advert featured a striking black and white image of a notable individual, such as Albert Einstein or Martin Luther King Jr., accompanied by the Apple logo. This simple yet powerful visual presentation created a sense of intrigue and curiosity.

- **Tagline and Brand Philosophy:** The tagline, 'Think Different', encapsulated Apple's brand philosophy and the company's commitment to innovation and creativity. It conveyed a powerful message that Apple's products empower individuals to break barriers, challenge norms, and think outside the box. The tagline resonated with individuals who aspired to make a difference and align themselves with a forward-thinking brand.

- **Celebrity Endorsement:** The use of influential figures from various fields, known for their groundbreaking achievements, added credibility and relevance to the advert. By associating Apple with these esteemed personalities, the advert conveyed a message of excellence, creativity, and pushing the boundaries of what is possible.

- **Simplicity and Clarity:** The advert embraced simplicity and clarity in its messaging. The absence of excessive text or clutter allowed the imagery and tagline to take centre stage, ensuring that the core message remained clear and impactful. This approach resonated with readers by presenting a concise and powerful statement.

- **Emotional Connection:** The advert successfully created an emotional connection by appealing to the aspirations and values of its target audience. It inspired individuals to think differently, challenge conventions, and embrace their unique perspectives. This emotional appeal fostered a sense of loyalty and admiration towards Apple as a brand that celebrated individuality and non-conformity.

- **Iconic Brand Identity:** Apple's branding was strategically positioned within the print advert. The prominent display of the Apple logo reinforced the brand's identity and immediate recognition. The advert's design consistency with Apple's overall visual style further solidified its association with innovation, elegance, and technological excellence.

Print advertising is a versatile medium that can effectively reach broad audiences and pinpoints niche groups.

See also:

Marketing Fundamentals: Marketing Budget
Market Analysis: Consumer Profiling
Market Analysis: Insights
Brand Building: Brand Positioning
Marketing Communication: Copywriting
Marketing Measurement: Data Analysis
Marketing Measurement: Key Performance Indicators

Chapter 36

Out-Of-Home Advertising

Out-of-home advertising, or outdoor advertising, is a marketing strategy that uses physical media to reach consumers outside their homes. This type of advertising includes billboards, transit advertising, street furniture advertising, and other creative outdoor displays. In the following chapter, we'll outline the benefits and limitations of OOH, how to set up an OOH campaign, and the different types of OOH based on objectives.

Characteristics of OOH

- **Reaching a large and diverse audience:** Out-of-home advertising can reach a vast and diverse audience, effectively building brand awareness. Billboards, for example, can be placed in high-traffic areas, such as busy roads, highways, and city centres, ensuring maximum exposure to a large audience. This advertising type can also target specific demographics, such as commuters, tourists, or pedestrians.

- **Creating a lasting impression:** Out-of-home has reach and can create a lasting impression on consumers. By designing them as eye-catching and memorable, consumers will remember and recall the ad later.

- **Targeting specific locations and demographics:** Out-of-home advertising can target specific locations and demographics. For example, transit advertising can target commuters on buses, trains, and subways, while street furniture advertising can target pedestrians in urban areas. Advertisers can tailor their messaging to specific audiences, increasing the ad campaign's effectiveness.

Despite the benefits of out-of-home advertising, there are also some limitations to consider:

- **Limited time exposure:** While out-of-home advertising can create a lasting impression, it is limited in terms of exposure time. Consumers may only see the ad for a few seconds, meaning the messaging needs to be concise and effective. Furthermore, consumers may not be able to engage with the ad like they can with digital or print ads.

- **Limited targeting options:** While out-of-home advertising can target specific locations and demographics, it is not as targeted as other forms of advertising, such as social media or search engine marketing. Advertisers may not be able to track consumer engagement in the same way they can with digital ads, so it may be more difficult to measure the ad campaign's effectiveness.

- **Limited creative options:** While out-of-home advertising can be designed to be eye-catching and memorable, there are some limitations to the creative options available. For example, billboards are limited in size and shape, so advertisers may be unable to use certain creative elements, such as video or animation.

Types of Out-of-Home Advertising

There are several types of out-of-home advertising, each with unique benefits and target audience. Knowing the different kinds can help companies choose the most effective medium for their advertising campaign. Here are some of the most common types and when to use them.

- **Billboards** are large, static advertising displays typically placed in high-traffic areas like highways or busy city streets. They are great for reaching a broad audience and generating brand awareness.

- **Transit advertising** refers to advertising on public transportation such as buses, trains, or subway stations. This medium is excellent for reaching commuters and travellers who spend much time on public transportation.

- **Street furniture advertising** refers to advertising on objects such as bus shelters, benches, or kiosks. This type of advertising is excellent for reaching pedestrians and can be effective for local businesses targeting specific neighbourhoods or communities.

- **Digital out-of-home advertising** involves digital displays in public places such as airports, shopping malls, or sports arenas. This medium offers the ability to create dynamic and interactive ads that engage the audience and generate interest.

- **Guerilla advertising** is a creative, non-traditional form designed to surprise and engage the audience. Examples include flash mobs or street installations. This type of advertising is great for generating buzz and going viral on social media.

Setting up an OOH Campaign

Developing an out-of-home advertising campaign can be daunting. Still, with a few key steps, businesses can create impactful campaigns that reach target audiences and achieve marketing goals.

1. **Define the target audience:** The first step in creating any advertising campaign is identifying the target audience. Consider demographics such as age, gender, location, and interests. This will help determine the most effective Out-of-home advertising medium to reach the target audience.

2. **Set campaign goals:** Define what the business wants to achieve with the Out-of-home advertising campaign. Should it increase brand awareness, drive sales, or promote a new product or service? By setting clear campaign goals, the Marketing Manager can ensure the campaign is focused and effective.

3. **Choose the suitable out-of-home advertising medium:** There are various Out-of-home advertising mediums, such as billboards, transit advertising, and street furniture advertising. Consider which medium is most effective for the target audience and campaign goals.

4. **Design an eye-catching ad:** Out-of-home advertising should be memorable. Use high-quality graphics and bold

text to grab attention. Keep the message concise and easy to read, as consumers only have a few seconds to view the ad.

5. **Select the right location:** The location of out-of-home advertising placement is crucial. Consider high-traffic areas where the target audience is likely to see the ad. Choose a location visible from a distance, such as a busy road or intersection.

6. **Measure campaign success:** After launching an out-of-home advertising campaign, it is important to measure its success. This can be done through impressions, engagement, and sales metrics. Use this data to refine future campaigns and improve their effectiveness.

Out-of-home is a great medium to reach a broad and localised set of customers.

See also:

Marketing Fundamentals: Marketing Budget
Market Analysis: Consumer Profiling
Market Analysis: Insights
Brand Building: Brand Positioning
Marketing Communication: Copywriting
Marketing Measurement: Data Analysis
Marketing Measurement: Key Performance Indicators

Chapter 37

Radio Advertising

Radio advertising has been a vital marketing tool for businesses worldwide, offering a unique platform to reach a diverse audience. Around the world, the effectiveness of radio advertising has stood the test of time, providing a reliable and cost-effective means to promote products and services. Here we will delve into why radio advertising is effective, explore the different types of broadcasting channels available, and highlight the key elements that make a radio ad successful.

History of Radio Advertising

Radio advertising has a rich history that spans over a century, evolving from its early experimental days to becoming a dominant force in advertising.

In the early 20th century, radio emerged as a groundbreaking technology, captivating audiences and opening new avenues for communication and entertainment. As radio broadcasting gained popularity, advertisers recognised its immense potential to reach a wide audience. In Britain, the first radio advertisement aired on 2 November 1922, marking the beginning of a new era in advertising.

The 1930s and 1940s witnessed the Golden Age of Radio, a period marked by increased commercialisation and innovation in radio advertising. Advertisers began creating bespoke radio programs, known as sponsored shows, where they would integrate their brands directly into the content. This approach allowed advertisers to engage listeners more immersive and entertainingly.

The 1950s and 1960s saw the rise of commercial broadcasting. The emergence of television as a dominant medium led to a shift in advertising focus, with radio advertising experiencing a decline in prominence. However, radio adapted to the changing landscape by offering more targeted programming and refining its advertising strategies to remain relevant.

The advent of the digital age brought about significant changes in radio advertising. The introduction of digital audio broadcasting (DAB) and online streaming platforms provided new opportunities for advertisers to engage with their target audience. Advertisers could now leverage data-driven insights and precise targeting to deliver tailored messages to listeners, enhancing the effectiveness of radio advertising campaigns.

The integration of radio and digital media platforms has further transformed the landscape of radio advertising. With the proliferation of smartphones and the increasing popularity of podcasting, advertisers can now reach listeners beyond traditional broadcast channels. This convergence has led to the emergence of dynamic and interactive radio ads, enabling real-time engagement and measurement.

As technology continues to evolve, radio advertising is poised to undergo further transformations. Voice-activated smart devices, such as smart speakers and virtual assistants, are reshaping the way people consume audio content. Advertisers are exploring opportunities in this realm, aiming to deliver personalised and contextually relevant ads to listeners.

The Effectiveness of Radio Advertising

Radio advertising continues to be a powerful medium, captivating audiences with its inherent strengths. Despite the rise of digital media, radio remains an influential platform for businesses due to the following reasons:

- **Wide Audience Reach:** Radio has a broad listenership, making it an ideal channel to reach a diverse range of consumers. According to the latest statistics, approximately 89% of the UK population tunes in to the radio every week, accounting for millions of potential customers across various demographics.

- **Targeted Marketing:** Radio stations cater to specific audiences, allowing advertisers to tailor their messages accordingly. With numerous stations focusing on specific music genres, age groups, or regional preferences, advertisers can align their ads with relevant programming, increasing the likelihood of reaching their target market effectively.

- **Cost-Effectiveness:** Compared to other forms of media, radio advertising offers a cost-effective solution for businesses with limited marketing budgets. It provides the opportunity to generate a high return on investment (ROI) by reaching a large audience at a fraction of the cost associated with television or print advertising.

Types of Broadcasting Channels

Radio advertising encompasses various broadcasting channels, each with its own unique characteristics. The following are the main types of radio broadcasting channels available:

- **National Radio:** National radio stations, such as BBC Radio 1, BBC Radio 2 in the UK, and commercial stations, like

Classic FM, have wide coverage nationwide. These channels attract millions of listeners and are suitable for advertisers with national campaigns or those targeting a broad audience.

- **Regional and Local Radio:** Regional and local radio stations serve specific geographical areas, making them ideal for businesses targeting a particular region or community. These stations provide advertisers with a more localised approach, enabling them to tailor their messages to suit the preferences and characteristics of the local audience.

- **Digital Radio:** Digital radio, including DAB (Digital Audio Broadcasting) and online streaming platforms, has gained significant popularity in recent years. This medium offers advertisers the advantage of precise targeting, as they can select specific digital stations or streaming services that align with their target market, ensuring a higher level of engagement and relevance.

Elements of a Successful Radio Ad

Creating an effective radio ad involves a careful combination of elements that captivate listeners and drive the desired response. The following are key factors that contribute to the success of a radio advertisement:

- **Engaging Storytelling:** A compelling narrative or story can hook listeners' attention and leave a lasting impression. An effective radio ad should evoke emotions, grab the audience's interest, and align with the brand's identity.

- **Memorable Jingles or Sound Effects:** Catchy jingles or unique sound effects can help make an ad more memorable. By incorporating distinct audio elements, businesses can create a strong brand identity and enhance their message recall.

- **Clear and Concise Message:** Radio ads have limited time to convey their message. Therefore, it is crucial to deliver the key information in a concise and straightforward manner. A clear call-to-action should be included to guide listeners towards the desired response, whether it be visiting a website, making a purchase, or attending an event.

- **Effective Use of Voiceover and Sound Quality:** The choice of voiceover artist and the overall sound quality can greatly influence the effectiveness of a radio ad. A skilled voiceover artist can bring life to the script, capturing the essence of the brand and engaging the audience. Additionally, ensuring high-quality sound production is essential to maintain clarity and professionalism, creating a positive listening experience.

- **Frequency and Timing:** Repetition plays a crucial role in radio advertising. By airing an ad multiple times, businesses increase the chances of reaching their target audience and reinforcing brand awareness. Additionally, selecting the appropriate time slots to air ads, such as during peak commuting hours or specific program segments, can maximise exposure to the intended audience.

- **Measurement and Analysis:** To gauge the effectiveness of a radio advertising campaign, it is vital to employ tracking mechanisms and analytics tools. Monitoring metrics such as reach, frequency, response rates, and customer feedback helps evaluate the impact of the ad and make necessary adjustments for future campaigns.

Audio Branding

Audio branding, also known as sonic branding or sound branding, refers to the strategic use of sound elements to create a distinctive and memorable brand identity. Just as visual elements like logos and colours evoke brand associations, audio elements such as jingles, melodies, or sound effects can trigger immediate recognition and emotional connections with consumers.

Understanding Audio Branding

Audio branding involves the intentional creation and deployment of sound elements that align with a brand's values, personality, and target audience. It aims to evoke emotions, enhance brand recognition, and create a consistent and cohesive brand experience across various touchpoints.

- **Jingles and Melodies:** Jingles are short, catchy tunes often accompanied by lyrics that encapsulate the essence of a brand. They serve as mnemonic devices, leaving a lasting impression in the minds of consumers. Melodies, even without lyrics, can also be used to evoke a specific mood or create brand associations.

- **Sound Effects:** Certain brands incorporate unique sound effects into their audio branding strategy. These sound effects, such as the iconic 'pop' sound when opening a can of

Coke or the Intel Inside jingle, become synonymous with the brand and instantly trigger brand recognition.

- **Voiceovers:** The voiceover element in audio branding involves selecting a specific voice or voice actor to represent the brand. This voice becomes an auditory representation of the brand's personality, conveying its values and establishing a connection with consumers.

Examples of Famous Signature Audio Branding

- **The Intel Corporation** is renowned for its signature audio branding, the Intel Inside jingle. Composed of five distinctive notes, this audio logo is widely recognized and associated with the brand. The short melody evokes a sense of reliability, innovation, and technological prowess.

- **McDonald's**, the global fast-food chain, has a notable audio branding strategy. Their famous 'I'm Lovin' It' jingle, created in collaboration with Pharrell Williams, has become deeply ingrained in popular culture. The upbeat melody and catchy lyrics reinforce the brand's positive and enjoyable experience.

- **Nokia**, once a dominant player in the mobile phone industry, incorporated an iconic audio branding element. The Nokia Tune, originally derived from the 19th-century guitar composition 'Gran Vals' by Francisco Tarrega, became synonymous with Nokia phones and triggered instant brand association.

- **Microsoft's Windows** operating system features an instantly recognizable audio logo. The four-second start-up sound, composed by Brian Eno, has evolved over the years, but its purpose remains the same—to signify the successful booting of the Windows platform and create a sense of familiarity and anticipation.

- **Skype,** the widely used communication platform, employs a distinctive audio branding element—the Skype ringtone. The ringing sound, unique to Skype, signifies incoming calls and has become a familiar and reassuring sound for millions of users around the world.

Radio is a particularly powerful tool for brands with strong sonic branding.

See also:

Marketing Fundamentals: Marketing Budget
Market Analysis: Consumer Profiling
Market Analysis: Insights
Brand Building: Brand Positioning
Marketing Communication: Copywriting
Marketing Measurement: Data Analysis
Marketing Measurement: Key Performance Indicators

Chapter 38

Public Relations

Public Relations (PR) is the practice of building and maintaining relationships between an organisation and its target audience, stakeholders, and the public. It involves strategically managing information and communication to promote a positive image of the organisation and its products or services. PR can encompass a range of activities, including media relations, social media management, event planning, crisis management, and reputation management.

Critics of PR often cite the fact that this channel does not always result in 100% positive coverage, unlimited media coverage, overnight brand recognition, instantaneous results, or even allows a company to have complete control over their media coverage. That is correct. However, it is important to understand that PR is an important part of any long-term strategy, not a stand-alone solution and that measurement of success often goes beyond immediate ROI.

Benefits of PR

Enhances Brand Awareness

PR can create buzz around an organisation and its products or services, through which a business can increase brand visibility and recognition by generating media coverage and leveraging social media. This helps establish the organisation as a leader in its industry and creates a competitive advantage.

Builds Credibility and Trust

Building credibility and trust with the target audience are incredibly important for any business. One of PR's primary functions is to create a positive image and reputation by promoting positive news and stories about the organisation, its products, and services, increasing sales and revenue in the process.

Creates Thought Leadership

Depending on the industry and product, businesses might want to establish themselves as thought leaders in their niche. Through PR, companies can position the organisation as a go-to source for information and insights by providing expert commentary and opinions on industry trends and issues. This can build credibility and trust with the target audience and create a competitive advantage.

Increases in Media Exposure

Media coverage is not always a given and is often the result of carefully planned PR campaigns. By generating media coverage for an organisation and its products or services, a business can increase exposure to the target audience and create new opportunities for growth and expansion. The key here is to leverage media relationships and craft compelling stories.

Manages Crisis Communications

PR can help to manage crisis communications and protect an organisation's reputation. In a crisis, such as a product recall or negative media coverage, PR can help mitigate the damage and maintain a positive image. PR can restore trust and credibility by communicating effectively with the target audience and stakeholders.

Designing a PR Campaign

Running PR campaigns is a popular marketing communication tool for many companies due to the benefits outlined previously. As with all campaigns, it's important to follow key steps to ensure the drive delivers on the initial objectives.

Step 1: Identify the Target Audience

The first step in designing a successful PR campaign is identifying the target audience. This involves understanding who the organisation is trying to reach and their needs and interests. This information will inform the development of key messages and the selection of media channels.

Step 2: Set Campaign Goals

The next step is to set campaign goals. This involves identifying what the organisation hopes to achieve through the PR campaign, such as increasing brand awareness, generating media coverage, or establishing thought leadership. These goals should be specific, measurable, and realistic.

Step 3: Craft Key Messages

Once the target audience and campaign goals have been identified, the next step is to craft key messages. These messages should be tailored to the target audience and communicate the organisation's value proposition and unique selling points. Key messages should be concise, memorable, and easy to understand.

Step 4: Develop Media Relationships

Developing media relationships is critical to a successful PR campaign. This involves identifying relevant journalists, bloggers, and influencers and building relationships with them. This can be done through targeted outreach, such as personalised emails and social media engagement.

Step 5: Measure Results

The final step in designing a successful PR campaign is to measure results. This involves tracking key metrics, such as media coverage, website traffic, and social media engagement. This information can be used to refine the campaign and optimise future PR efforts.

Example PR Campaign: Launching a New Product

To illustrate how these steps can be applied in practice, let's consider an example PR campaign for launching a new product. Here's how the steps might look:

Step 1: Identify the Target Audience

The target audience for the new product is women aged 25-45 who are interested in health and wellness.

Step 2: Set Campaign Goals

The goals for the PR campaign are to generate media coverage in relevant health and wellness publications, establish the organisation as a thought leader in the industry, and increase website traffic and product sales.

Step 3: Craft Key Messages

The key messages for the PR campaign are:

- The new product is a breakthrough in natural health and wellness.
- The new product is backed by science and research.
- The new product is designed specifically for women.

Step 4: Develop Media Relationships

The organisation will develop relationships with health and wellness journalists and bloggers by providing them early access to the new product and offering expert commentary on health and wellness topics.

Step 5: Plan PR Tactics

The next step in the PR campaign is to plan tactics to help achieve the campaign goals. For the example PR campaign of launching a new product, the tactics could include:

- Hosting a launch event: This can generate media coverage and create buzz around the new product. The event can include product demos, expert speakers, and media interviews.

- Pitching media outlets: The organisation can pitch relevant media outlets with a press release or media kit that includes information about the new product, expert commentary, and images.

- Engaging social media influencers: The organisation can partner with influencers with a large following in the health and wellness space. These influencers can share their experience with the new product and provide testimonials.

- Creating content: The organisation can create content that promotes the new product and provides value to the target audience. This can include blog posts, infographics, and videos.

Step 6: Execute the PR Campaign

The next step is to execute the PR campaign. This involves implementing the planned tactics and building relationships with journalists, bloggers, and influencers. The organisation should track the results of each tactic and adjust the campaign as needed.

Step 7: Evaluate the PR Campaign

The final step is to evaluate the PR campaign. This involves measuring the campaign's results against the set goals and objectives. The organisation should analyse media coverage, website traffic, social media engagement, and sales to determine the campaign's success. The lessons learned from this evaluation can be used to improve future PR campaigns.

PR is a key tool for building and maintaining customer relationships and increasing brand awareness.

See also:

Marketing Fundamentals: Marketing Budget
Market Analysis: Consumer Profiling
Market Analysis: Insights
Brand Building: Brand Positioning
Marketing Communication: Copywriting
Marketing Measurement: Data Analysis
Marketing Measurement: Key Performance Indicators

Chapter 39

Word-Of-Mouth Advertising

Word-of-mouth (WOM) marketing is one of the oldest and most effective forms of marketing. It is a powerful way to spread brand, product, or service information and occurs when people talk about a product or service to others, often recommending it to them. In this section, we will explore the importance of word-of-mouth marketing, how it works, and how businesses can build a successful campaign.

Importance of Word-of-Mouth Marketing

Word-of-mouth marketing is an effective way to reach new customers, as when people recommend a product or service to others, it creates trust and credibility. People are more likely to trust a recommendation from a friend or family member than an advertisement. Word-of-mouth marketing is also cost-effective, as it does not require a large budget for advertising. It can be a valuable tool for small businesses looking to increase their customer base without spending much money.

How Word-of-Mouth Marketing Works

When customers have a positive experience with a product or service, they are likelier to talk about it with their friends and family. This can lead to a chain reaction of recommendations as more people hear about the product or service and decide to try it themselves.

Businesses can also incentivise word-of-mouth marketing by offering referral programs or discounts to customers who recommend their product or service to others. This encourages customers to discuss the product or service and can increase sales.

Components of a Successful Word-of-Mouth Campaign

- **Create a Memorable Experience:** This can be achieved by providing exceptional customer service, offering unique products or services, or creating a personalised experience for each customer.

- **Encourage Customer Feedback:** By asking customers for their opinion, businesses can learn what works well and what needs improvement. This feedback can also be used to create better products or services that will encourage customers to recommend them to others.

- **Build a Strong Online Presence:** This can be achieved by creating a website and social media accounts and engaging with customers online. By being active on social media and responding to customer inquiries, businesses can create a positive reputation and encourage customers to recommend their products or service to others.

- **Offer Incentives for Referrals:** This can include discounts, free products or services, or other rewards. By offering incentives, businesses can encourage customers to recommend their product or service to others and increase their customer base.

Tracking Word-of-Mouth Recommendations

More than for almost any other type of communication channel, time is of the essence. Whether the word-of-mouth campaign is initiated by the brand on purpose or people naturally advocate for the product without immediate incentives, it's on the brand to react quickly to amplify the reaction and drive awareness. To do that, companies can access various tools to track what consumers say about them.

- **Social Media Listening:** Regularly monitor social media platforms, including Twitter, Facebook, Instagram, and LinkedIn, for mentions of your product. Use social listening tools to track relevant keywords, hashtags, and brand mentions. Engage with users discussing your product and address any concerns or questions they may have.

- **Set up Google Alerts:** Create Google Alerts for your product name, brand, and related keywords. Google will send you notifications whenever these keywords appear in online discussions, blog posts, news articles, or forums.

- **Online Review Sites:** Keep an eye on popular review sites like Yelp, Google Reviews, and industry-specific platforms where customers might leave feedback about your product. Respond to reviews, both positive and negative, to show that you value customer feedback.

- **Customer Surveys and Feedback:** Implement customer satisfaction surveys and feedback forms on your website, email newsletters, or purchase confirmation pages. Include open-ended questions that encourage customers to share their experiences and recommend your product to others.

- **Referral Programs and Tracking Codes:** Offer referral programs to incentivise your existing customers to refer others to your product. Use unique referral codes or tracking links to track referrals and identify which customers are recommending your product.

- **Influencer Partnerships:** Collaborate with influencers and brand ambassadors who can spread word-of-mouth recommendations about your product to their followers. Track their posts, mentions, and engagement to gauge the impact of their recommendations.

- **Customer Support and Service Channels:** Monitor customer support channels such as emails, live chats, and phone calls for mentions or word-of-mouth recommendations. Keep track of any positive feedback or testimonials shared by customers during these interactions.

- **Industry Forums and Communities:** Participate in online communities, industry forums, and social media groups where discussions related to your product are taking place. Engage with users, answer questions, and address concerns to build trust and encourage positive recommendations.

- **Competitive Analysis:** Keep an eye on your competitors' online presence and social media platforms. By monitoring their word-of-mouth recommendations, you can gain insights into what they are doing well or areas where they fall short, allowing you to refine your own product and marketing strategies.

Examples of Successful Word-of-Mouth Campaigns

- **Airbnb:** Airbnb is a home-sharing platform allowing users to rent their homes to travellers. The company's successful word-of-mouth campaign was built on creating a memorable customer experience. By offering unique and personalised accommodations, Airbnb made a positive reputation that encouraged customers to recommend the service to others.

- **Glossier:** Glossier is a beauty brand that sells skincare and makeup products. The company's successful word-of-mouth campaign was built on building a strong online presence. By engaging with customers on social media and creating a community around their brand, Glossier created a positive reputation and encouraged customers to try their products.

Word-of-mouth is a powerful method to utilise a brand's customer base to drive sales.

See also:

Market Analysis: Consumer Profiling
Market Analysis: Insights
Brand Building: Brand Positioning
Marketing Measurement: Data Analysis
Marketing Measurement: Key Performance Indicators

Chapter 40

Influencer Marketing

Influencer marketing involves collaborating with influential people in the company's industry or niche to promote products or services. Influencers have a large following and can sway their followers' purchasing decisions. This type of activity is most effective when the objective is to reach highly engaged audiences, increase brand awareness, and drive sales. In this chapter, we will outline the types of partnerships brands can enter to collaborate with influencers, the types of influencers that there are, how to choose them according to the business's campaign objective, how to set up an influencer campaign, and how to write an influencer brief.

Influencer and Brand Partnership Types

Influencer marketing has its roots in celebrity endorsements, which have been used in advertising since the early 20th century. However, the rise of social media platforms such as YouTube, Instagram, and TikTok has transformed influencer marketing into a distinct form of marketing in its own right.

Influencer marketing can take many forms, making it highly flexible to adjust to the brand's goals, target audience, and budget. Here are some of the most common types of influencer marketing:

- **Sponsored content:** This involves paying an influencer to create and share content promoting a brand's product or service. This can be a sponsored blog post, YouTube video, Instagram post, or other social media content.

- **Product reviews:** Here an influencer receives a product from a brand to try out and share their honest opinion with their audience. This type of campaign can be particularly effective for driving sales, as consumers often rely on product reviews before purchasing.

- **Brand ambassadorship:** Arguably, one of the most effective ways to work with influencers is to make them long-term brand partners and allow them to promote products or services over an extended period. This campaign can effectively build brand awareness and loyalty among the influencer's followers.

- **Affiliate marketing:** This format allows the influencer to promote a brand's product or service and receive a commission on any sales that result from their promotion. This can be an effective way to drive sales and generate revenue for both the brand and the influencer.

- **Guest content:** This tactic involves collaborating with influencers to create content for a brand's website or social media channels, such as blog posts, videos, or social media takeovers. These campaigns can effectively increase brand visibility and drive website traffic.

- **Event sponsorship:** This describes partnering with an influencer to sponsor an event or experience. These campaigns are often executed when brands want to generate buzz and reach a highly targeted audience.

- **Influencer contests:** Influencers promote a brand's products or services to their followers and encourage them to participate in a contest or giveaway. This can be an effective way to generate engagement and drive sales.

Influencer Tiers

There are several different types of influencers that brands can work with for their marketing campaigns. Choosing the right type of influencer will depend on the brand's goals, target audience, and budget. Here are some of the most common types of influencers and how they can be used for different marketing objectives:

- **Celebrity influencers:** Often well-known public figures with a large following. They can effectively increase brand awareness and reach, as their followers are often fans interested in their personal lives and activities. Celebrity influencers can be expensive, but they can be effective for launching new products or generating buzz around a brand.

- **Macro-influencers:** The second-biggest tier of online personalities have a following of between 100,000 and 1 million followers on social media. They can be effective in reaching a broad audience and generating brand awareness. Macro influencers can be less expensive to work with than celebrity influencers, and they can effectively promote new products or services.

- **Micro-influencers:** This tier of influencers has a following of between 1,000 and 100,000 followers on social media. They can be effective for reaching a highly targeted audience and generating engagement. Micro-influencers are often experts in their niche or industry, and their followers trust their recommendations. They can effectively promote niche products or services and generate user-generated content.

- **Nano-influencers:** These Creators have a following of less than 1,000 followers on social media. They can effectively generate local buzz and build brand loyalty among a highly engaged audience. Nano-influencers are often friends, family members, or colleagues and can effectively promote small businesses or local events.

- **Industry experts:** These personalities are highly knowledgeable and respected influencers in their industry or niche. They can be effective for building brand credibility and generating thought leadership. Industry experts can effectively promote B2B products or services and generate high-quality leads.

How to Set up Influencer Campaigns

Writing an effective brief is essential to delivering a successful campaign. Especially when working with Influencers, it's important to communicate the expectations of the partnership, as the business is giving up control of how its brand is portrayed to potential new and existing customers.

Set campaign goals: The first step in designing an influencer campaign is to set clear goals. Is it about increasing brand awareness, driving sales, or promoting a new product or service? Defining the goals will help to determine the most effective influencer marketing strategy.

Identify the business's target audience: Identify the target audience and determine which influencers they follow. This will help choose the right influencers to collaborate with and ensure that the campaign effectively reaches the intended target audience.

Choose the right influencers: Choosing the right influencers is key to the success of the influencer campaign. Look for influencers with a large, engaged following in the industry or niche. Consider their demographics, reach, engagement rate, and authenticity. Some companies use influencer marketing platforms or agency services to find and vet potential influencers.

Determine the collaboration type: There are several influencer collaborations, including sponsored posts, product reviews, and affiliate partnerships. Determine which collaboration is most effective for the campaign goals and budget.

Set campaign budget: Influencer marketing can range in cost, depending on the size of the influencer's following and the type of collaboration. Set a budget for the campaign that aligns with the campaign goals earlier. Depending on the platform and campaign, there is the option to compensate partners per content piece, affiliate link sales, or monthly if it's a longer agreement.

Create engaging content: Collaborate with the influencer to create engaging content that resonates with their audience and aligns with the brand. Brands should treat their partners as creative directors, allowing them to feedback on what content will work best on their channel based on previous experiences and the knowledge of their audience. Ensure the content is visually appealing and includes a clear call to action that encourages their followers to engage with the brand.

Track and measure campaign success: After launching the campaign, tracking and measuring its success is important. Use reach, engagement, and sales metrics to determine the campaign's effectiveness. Use this data to refine future campaigns and improve their effectiveness.

The success of an influencer campaign is directly correlated to the synergies created between the brand and chosen personality.

See also:

Marketing Fundamentals: Marketing Budget
Market Analysis: Consumer Profiling
Market Analysis: Insights
Brand Building: Brand Positioning
Marketing Communication: Copywriting
Marketing Measurement: Data Analysis
Marketing Measurement: Key Performance Indicators

Chapter 41

Email Marketing

Email marketing is a powerful tool for businesses to reach and engage customers. It involves sending promotional messages or newsletters to a list of subscribers who have opted in to receive communications from the company. With the right approach and strategy, email marketing can help businesses to build brand awareness, drive sales, and foster customer relationships. Here, we'll take a closer look at email marketing and its most important components.

Benefits of Email Marketing

Email marketing is a highly effective digital marketing strategy that sends targeted messages and promotional content via email to recipients who have voluntarily subscribed to receive such communications. Here are some key benefits of using this communication channel:

- **Cost-effective:** Email marketing is generally considered a cost-effective marketing channel compared to other forms of advertising. There are no printing or postage costs associated with email marketing, making it an affordable option for businesses of all sizes.

- **Broad Reach:** Email allows businesses to reach a large audience instantly. With the ability to send emails to thousands or even millions of subscribers, companies can quickly disseminate information, promotions, and updates to a broad audience.

- **Targeted Audience:** This channel allows businesses to target specific audience segments with personalised content. By segmenting email lists based on demographics, customer behaviour, or preferences, businesses can tailor their messages to be more relevant and engaging, leading to higher open and click-through rates.

- **Relationship Building:** Regularly sending valuable content and relevant offers to subscribers can help build trust and loyalty, increasing customer retention and repeat business.

- **Increased Engagement:** Subscribers who have voluntarily opted in to receive emails are more likely to be receptive to the messages they receive, leading to higher open rates, click-through rates, and conversion rates than other advertising forms.

- **Measurable Results:** Email marketing provides businesses with valuable data and insights, allowing them to measure the success of their campaigns. Metrics such as open rates, click-through rates, conversion rates, and subscriber engagement can be tracked and analysed, providing businesses with valuable feedback on their marketing efforts.

- **Automation and Personalisation:** Emails allow for high automation, enabling businesses to send targeted messages to subscribers at the right time with relevant content. This helps save time and effort while delivering more personalised experiences to subscribers, leading to better engagement and results.

- **Flexibility and Creativity:** From newsletters and promotions to surveys and event invitations, businesses can use email marketing to deliver a wide range of content to suit their marketing goals and objectives.

How to Build a Newsletter

Building an Email List

Before a business can start sending emails to customers, it needs to have a list of subscribers. There are a few different ways to build an email list, but the most effective method is offering something valuable in exchange for a person's contact information. This might include a free e-book, discount code, or access to exclusive content. One can also encourage website visitors to subscribe to the email list by adding a sign-up form to the website or blog.

Segmenting the List

Once a list is built, it's important to segment the subscribers based on their interests, behaviour, and demographics. This creates targeted and personalised messages more likely to resonate with each subscriber. For example, one might segment the list based on the products or services a subscriber has purchased, or their location or age.

Crafting Engaging Email Content

The content of the emails is crucial to the success of any email marketing campaign. The aim is to create engaging, informative, and relevant content for subscribers. This might include product updates, industry news, or tips and advice related to the business. It's also essential to include calls-to-action (CTAs) in the emails, encouraging subscribers to take specific actions, such as purchasing or visiting the company's website.

Email Design

The design of the emails is also important. Emails should be visually appealing and easily read on any device, including desktops, laptops, and mobile devices. This might involve using a template or creating a custom design that reflects the brand and messaging. It's also essential to include images and graphics in the emails to break up the text and make the messages more engaging.

Automating Emails

Email automation allows businesses to send targeted messages to subscribers at specific times or based on particular actions. For example, one might set up an automated welcome email to new subscribers when they first sign up. Automated emails can also be triggered by specific actions, such as purchasing or abandoning a cart on the website. Automation can help to save time and ensure subscribers receive relevant messages at the right time.

Measuring Results

One of the most critical components of email marketing is measuring the results. This allows us to see what is working and what is not so that adjustments can be made and campaigns are improved over time. The key metrics to track include open, click-through, conversion, and unsubscribe rates. By analysing these metrics, one can gain insights into the effectiveness of the emails and make data-driven decisions about one's email marketing strategy.

Example of an Email Campaign

Let's review an example email marketing campaign by Nike, a global athletic footwear and apparel leader.

Campaign Objective

Promote a new product launch and drive sales among their subscriber base.

Campaign Strategy

- **Teaser Campaign:** Nike created a teaser campaign to generate excitement and anticipation among their email subscribers about an upcoming product launch. They sent teaser emails with intriguing subject lines, sneak peeks, and hints about the new product, creating curiosity and anticipation.

- **Exclusive Access:** Nike offered exclusive access to their email subscribers for pre-ordering the new product before it was available to the general public. This created a sense of exclusivity and urgency among subscribers, motivating them to take action and purchase.

- **Compelling Visuals and Copy:** Nike used high-quality visuals and persuasive copy in their emails to showcase the new product's features, benefits, and unique selling points. They also included customer testimonials and reviews to build trust and credibility and encourage recipients to consider purchasing.

- **Limited-Time Offer:** Nike included a limited-time offer in their emails, such as a discount or free shipping, to create a sense of urgency and drive immediate action. This encouraged subscribers to take advantage of the offer and purchase before it expired.

- **Cross-Channel Promotion:** Nike integrated their email campaign with other marketing channels, such as their website, social media, and in-store signage, to create a consistent and cohesive message about the new product launch. This helped to amplify the campaign and generate buzz among their audience.

- **Mobile Optimisation:** Nike ensured that their emails were optimised for mobile devices, as a significant portion of their audience accessed emails on mobile devices. This provided recipients with a seamless and user-friendly experience, leading to higher engagement and conversion rates.

Results

Nike's email marketing campaign for their new product launch resulted in impressive outcomes, including:

- High engagement among their subscriber base as evidenced by higher open rates, click-through rates, and overall interaction with the content.

- Increased sales and revenue from the pre-orders of the new product, as the exclusive access and limited-time offer motivated subscribers to make a purchase.

- Enhanced brand awareness and buzz as the teaser campaign and cross-channel promotion generated excitement and anticipation among their audience.

- Improved customer loyalty as the personalised and exclusive offer for email subscribers reinforced Nike's brand positioning and value proposition.

Email marketing can be a highly effective way to reach and engage with audiences, build relationships, and drive conversions.

See also:

Marketing Fundamentals: Marketing Budget
Market Analysis: Consumer Profiling
Market Analysis: Insights
Brand Building: Brand Positioning
Marketing Communication: Copywriting
Marketing Measurement: Data Analysis
Marketing Measurement: Key Performance Indicators

Chapter 42

Search Engine Optimisation

Search Engine Optimisation, or SEO, is vital to any business's online presence. It is related to optimising a company's website and content to rank higher on search engines like Google, Bing, and Yahoo. The higher the website ranks, the more visible it becomes to potential customers, translating into increased traffic, engagement, and revenue. SEO involves strategies and techniques to improve a website's organic search engine rankings.

How SEO Works

Search Engine Optimisation is fundamental for enhancing a website's visibility in search engine results. Google's EEAT methodology, which involves Experience, Expertise, Authoritativeness, and Trustworthiness, is vital in determining a website's ranking.

Experience aims to differentiate between AI-generated and human-generated content. It was introduced shortly after tools such as ChatGPT emerged. This factor is showcased by highlighting that there are real people behind a website, giving visitors the confidence to transact with a business. For example, this could be done via a well-thought-through 'About Us' page showcasing the team's credentials and qualifications.

Expertise revolves around the depth and breadth of knowledge showcased by a website's content creators. To optimise for expertise, websites should provide well-researched and accurate information relevant to their field. By presenting high-quality content written by subject-matter experts, websites are more likely to be acknowledged as authoritative by search engines.

Authoritativeness emphasises the credibility and reputation of a website. Websites can enhance their authoritativeness by acquiring backlinks from other reputable websites, which endorse their reliability and value. Consistently updating content and ensuring its alignment with industry standards further contributes to establishing authority.

Trustworthiness is essential for fostering user confidence. Websites should adopt transparent practices, clearly displaying contact information, privacy policies, and terms of service. User-generated content, such as reviews and testimonials, can also boost trustworthiness. Additionally, websites must provide secure browsing experiences by implementing HTTPS protocols and safeguarding user data.

By adhering to these principles, websites can enhance their visibility and achieve higher rankings in search engine results, ultimately driving more organic traffic.

Benefits of SEO

There are several benefits to implementing SEO strategies and techniques on the website:

- **Increased visibility:** Optimising a company's website for search engines can increase its visibility and attract more potential customers.

- **Higher rankings:** The higher the website ranks on search engines, the more likely it is to be clicked on by potential customers.

- **More traffic:** Increased visibility and higher rankings can translate into increased traffic to the website.

- **Improved user experience:** SEO can help improve the website's user experience by making it more accessible and user-friendly.

- **Increased revenue:** A company can increase revenue and grow its business by attracting more potential customers to the website.

SEO Practises

SEO comprises several key components, each with its specific objectives and techniques.

- **Keyword Research:** Keyword research identifies relevant and high-traffic keywords for which the company wants to rank on search engines. Keyword research helps understand what the target audience is searching for and what phrases should be targeted to attract them to the website.

- **On-Page Optimisation:** On-page optimisation includes all the elements on the website that can be optimised for search engines, such as title tags, meta descriptions, header tags, internal linking, and content optimisation. Optimising these elements can signal to search engines what the website is about and improve its chances of ranking higher.

- **Off-Page Optimization:** Off-page optimisation refers to activities outside one's website that can still impact the search engine rankings. This includes building high-quality backlinks, social media marketing, influencer outreach, and guest blogging. Off-page optimisation can help increase the website's authority and relevance, improving its search engine rankings.

- **Technical SEO:** Technical SEO refers to the technical aspects of the website that can impact its search engine rankings. This includes site speed, mobile responsiveness, URL structure, and architecture. Technical SEO can help search engines crawl and index the website more effectively, improving its visibility on search engine results pages (SERPs).

- **Local SEO:** Local SEO is a strategy to optimise the website and its content for local search results. This includes optimising the website's Google My Business listing, local citations, and online reviews. Local SEO can help improve the website's visibility for locally based searches, such as 'best coffee shop near me'.

SEO in Practice for Businesses

Conduct Keyword Research

Topic research stems from keyword research and is an essential step in developing a robust SEO strategy. While keyword research provides a solid starting point, it's through topic research that website owners can truly excel. Building comprehensive topic lists allows for content strategies that outperform those solely focused on keywords. This approach is especially vital considering Google's emphasis on human-focused contextual and semantic content analysis. Websites can establish higher topical authority in specific subjects by creating content centred around topics. This is often achieved through a 'Hubs and Spokes' approach, where key hubs are identified, and topic lists are developed to cover relevant keywords. By incorporating topic research into their SEO strategy, businesses can effectively bridge the gap between keyword research and creating high-quality, engaging content that resonates with their target audience. This enhances their visibility in search engine results and positions them as authoritative sources in their respective fields.

Optimise Website Structure

An optimised website structure is of paramount importance in SEO. Businesses must prioritise creating a user-friendly website, facilitating easy navigation and showcasing a clear page hierarchy. Implementing a sitemap is crucial, as it assists search engines in efficiently crawling and indexing the website's pages. Moreover, it is vital to ensure the website is mobile-friendly, considering the growing number of users accessing the internet through mobile devices. It is noteworthy that Googlebot, Google's web crawler, now follows a mobile-first approach, making mobile-friendliness a primary criterion for evaluating website performance. While this aspect falls more under on-page SEO than website structure, it significantly impacts search engine rankings and user experience. Therefore, businesses should prioritise responsive design and mobile optimisation to cater to the evolving browsing habits of users and align with Google's mobile-first indexing approach. By focusing on both website structure and on-page SEO, businesses can enhance their chances of attracting organic traffic, improving user engagement, and achieving higher rankings in search engine results.

Creating High-Quality Content

In the realm of SEO, content reigns supreme. Businesses must strongly emphasise crafting high-quality, valuable content that caters to their target audience's needs. This involves developing a diverse range of content types, such as blog posts, articles, and more, tailored to address the questions and concerns of potential customers. The content must be well-written, informative, and engaging, capturing reader attention and delivering meaningful insights. To create an effective content strategy, businesses can follow a typical approach that involves several key steps. First, they should identify the core 'hubs' or central themes relevant to their industry or niche. Then, for each hub, they can build comprehensive topic lists encompassing various subtopics and keywords. By analysing the top five results in search engine results pages (SERPs), businesses can determine the primary user intent behind each topic, whether it's informational, comparative, or transactional. With this insight, they can tailor their content strategy for each landing page type, utilising blog articles as a knowledge base, educational resources, or even transactional pages such as product descriptions, browse pages, or lead generation forms. By following this strategy, businesses can create a well-rounded content approach that addresses different stages of the user journey and establishes their authority in the industry.

Optimise On-Page Elements

On-page elements, including title tags, meta descriptions, and header tags, play a pivotal role in SEO. Businesses must optimise these elements according to their target keywords. Title tags should be descriptive and incorporate relevant keywords to represent the page's content accurately. Similarly, meta descriptions should be compelling and enticing, encouraging users to click through to the website. However, it is essential to note that Google often overrides these meta descriptions when discovering on-page content that provides a more fitting description. To address this, businesses should aim to create meta descriptions that align with the visible content on the page whenever possible. This ensures the meta description remains relevant and coherent, even if Google displays an alternate explanation. By optimising on-page elements thoughtfully and aligning them with the overall content, businesses can enhance their visibility in search engine results and attract organic traffic to their website.

Build Backlinks

Backlinks are links from other websites to the business's website. They are essential in SEO because search engines consider them a sign of trust and authority. Businesses should focus on building high-quality backlinks from relevant websites. They can do this by guest blogging, participating in online forums, and creating high-quality content that other websites will want to link to.

Monitor and Measure Results

Businesses should monitor and measure their SEO results regularly. Tools like Google Analytics and Search Console can track a website's performance, paying attention to organic traffic, bounce rate, and keyword rankings.

SEO is a vital tool for businesses to increase their visibility online.

See also:

Marketing Communication: Pay-Per-Click Advertising
Product Distribution: Online Marketplace
Product Distribution: eCommerce

Chapter 43

Pay-Per-Click Advertising

Pay-per-click advertising (PPC) is a powerful and cost-effective form of online advertising. It allows businesses to target their audience through search engines, social media platforms, and other websites. With PPC advertising, businesses only pay when someone clicks on their ad, making it a very efficient form of advertising. This overview will discuss PPC advertising, how it works, and its marketing benefits.

What is PPC Advertising?

PPC advertising is a digital marketing strategy that allows businesses to advertise their products or services to a targeted audience. It is a type of online advertising involving ads on search engines, social media platforms, or other websites. When a user clicks on an ad, the advertiser pays a fee to the platform or website that hosted the ad. The cost of the click varies depending on the competition for the targeted keywords and the ad's relevance to the user's search query.

PPC advertising is often associated with search engine advertising, as it is commonly used on search engines such as Google and Bing. These search engines offer advertising platforms such as Google Ads and Bing Ads, which allow businesses to create and manage their PPC ads. However, PPC ads are also available on social media platforms like Facebook, Instagram, Twitter, TikTok, and LinkedIn. These platforms offer advertising options that allow businesses to target their ads to specific audiences based on demographics, interests, and behaviour.

How does PPC Advertising work?

PPC advertising works on a bidding system. Advertisers bid on specific keywords or phrases they want to target with their ads. When a user types in a search query that matches the advertiser's keywords, the platform will show the highest bidder's ad in the search results. The advertiser only pays when the user clicks on their ad.

The bidding system is based on a combination of factors, including the maximum bid amount, the ad's quality score, and the ad's relevance to the user's search query. The quality score is a metric that determines the ad's quality, the landing page's relevance, and the user's experience. The higher the quality score, the more likely the ad will be displayed and the less the advertiser will pay per click.

PPC advertising allows businesses to target specific audiences based on demographics, interests, and behaviour. For example, a business selling pet supplies could target pet owners who have shown an interest in pet food, pet toys, or pet grooming products. This targeted approach ensures that the ads are displayed to the right audience, which increases the chances of conversion and reduces the cost per click.

Benefits of PPC Advertising for Marketing

The benefits of PPC advertising for marketing are numerous. When utilised effectively, PPC advertising can provide businesses with increased brand exposure, precise targeting options, cost control, immediate results, and valuable insights into customer behaviour.

Firstly, PPC advertising allows businesses to increase brand exposure by appearing at the top of search engine results pages (SERPs) or other relevant websites. This heightened visibility can help create brand awareness and improve brand recall among potential customers, increasing brand recognition and credibility.

Secondly, PPC advertising provides precise targeting options allowing businesses to narrow their audience based on location, demographics, interests, and online behaviour. This level of precision targeting ensures that ads are shown to the most relevant audience, increasing the likelihood of attracting qualified leads and driving conversions.

Thirdly, businesses can control their budget and set daily or monthly spending limits. They only pay when a user clicks on their ad, making it cost-effective and allowing them to measure their ROI accurately. Additionally, businesses can optimise their campaign by monitoring and adjusting their bids, keywords, and targeting options to maximise ad spending and achieve better results.

Furthermore, PPC advertising can deliver immediate results. Unlike other marketing channels that may take time to generate results, PPC ads can start driving traffic and conversions as soon as the campaign is launched. This makes PPC advertising ideal for businesses looking for quick and measurable results, especially for time-sensitive promotions or product launches.

Lastly, PPC advertising provides valuable insights into customer behaviour. Businesses can gather data on user engagement, click-through rates, conversion rates, and other key metrics through analytics and reporting tools. These insights can help businesses refine their marketing strategies, optimise their campaigns, and make data-driven decisions to improve their marketing performance.

How to Design a PPC Campaign

Step 1 Set Clear Campaign Objectives: The first step in designing a PPC campaign is to define clear objectives. This involves understanding the campaign's goals, whether it is to drive website traffic, generate leads, increase sales, or boost brand awareness. Setting specific and measurable objectives will provide a clear direction for the campaign and help track its success.

Step 2 Conduct Keyword Research: Keyword research is critical in PPC campaign design. It involves identifying the keywords and phrases relevant to the promoted business, products, or services. Businesses can use keyword research tools, such as Google Ads Keyword Planner, to identify high-volume and low-competition keywords to help them effectively reach their target audience.

Step 3 Create compelling creative assets: The next step is to create compelling ad assets that resonate with the target audience. Businesses should create concise, relevant ad copy and graphics highlighting unique selling propositions (USPs). Ad copy should also include a strong call-to-action (CTA) that encourages users to take the desired action, such as clicking on the ad or purchasing.

Step 4 Define Target Audience and Set Targeting Options: Defining the target audience is crucial in PPC campaign design. Businesses should identify their target audience based on demographics, location, interests, and online behaviour. This information will help them set specific targeting options within their PPC campaign, such as geographic, demographic, and audience targeting, to ensure their ads are shown to the most relevant audience.

Step 5 Set Budget and Bidding Strategy: Setting a budget and bidding strategy is crucial in PPC campaign design. Businesses should determine their budget for their campaign, and set a daily or monthly spending limit accordingly. They should also choose a bidding strategy, such as manual or automated, based on their campaign objectives and budget.

Step 6 Monitor and Optimize Campaign: Once the PPC campaign is launched, Businesses should regularly monitor its performance and make necessary optimisations. This includes reviewing key metrics such as click-through rates (CTR), conversion rates, and return on ad spend (ROAS) and adjusting keywords, ad copy, targeting options, and bidding strategy to improve campaign performance.

Step 7 Test and Refine Campaign: Testing and refining the PPC campaign is ongoing. Businesses should experiment with different ad variations, landing pages, targeting options, and bidding strategies to identify what works best for their campaign. They should also keep track of industry trends, competitor activities, and user behaviour to stay updated and make data-driven decisions for campaign refinement.

Example of a PPC Campaign

PPC can be a clever marketing tool that can drive an effective reach for brands. A great example of this is the campaign by the Dollar Shave Club.

Objective

Increase brand awareness and drive subscriptions for their monthly razor subscription service.

Campaign Strategy

- **Creative Ad Copy:** Dollar Shave Club used witty ad copy that stood out from the competition and resonated with its target audience. They incorporated clever wordplay, puns, and humour into their ad copy, making them memorable and shareable.

- **Bold Branding:** They used consistent and bold branding across their ads, landing pages, and website, with a distinctive logo and colour scheme that helped them stand out in a crowded market. They also used eye-catching visuals, including images of their razor products and before-and-after grooming transformations.

- **Unique Selling Proposition (USP):** Dollar Shave Club highlighted their unique selling proposition: the convenience of their monthly razor subscription service that delivers high-quality razors to customers' doors at an affordable price. They emphasised the benefits of their service, such as saving time and money and avoiding the hassle of purchasing razors in-store.

- **Humorous Video Ads:** They created humorous and viral video ads that went viral on social media platforms like YouTube, Facebook, and Instagram. These video ads featured the company's CEO delivering funny and entertaining pitches about their razor products and subscription service, which helped to generate buzz, shares, and engagement.

- **Audience Targeting:** Dollar Shave Club utilised precise audience targeting options, such as demographics, interests, and behaviour targeting, to reach their ideal customers interested in grooming, personal care, and subscription services. They also targeted specific keywords related to razors, shaving, and grooming to capture relevant search traffic.

- **Call-to-Action (CTA):** They used clear and compelling CTAs in their ad copy and landing pages, such as 'Get Started', 'Join Now', and 'Try it for $1', to encourage users to take action and sign up for their subscription service.

Results

Dollar Shave Club's clever PPC campaign was a huge success and helped them achieve remarkable results:

- Increased brand awareness and recognition, with their ads and videos being shared widely on social media and generating millions of views.

- Significant increase in subscriptions and customer base, with over 3 million subscribers within the first five years of their campaign.

- Positive impact on sales and revenue, with a reported valuation of over $1 billion within six years of launching their PPC campaign.

- Established themselves as a disruptive and innovative brand in the razor industry, challenging traditional razor brands and gaining a loyal following among their target audience.

PPC advertising is a targeted method to promote products or services and reach niche target audiences.

See also:

Marketing Fundamentals: Marketing Budget
Marketing Communication: Copywriting
Marketing Communication: Search Engine Optimisation
Marketing Measurement: Data Analysis
Marketing Measurement: Key Performance Indicators

VII

Product Distribution

Chapter 44

Brick & Mortar Retail Stores

Retail stores have long been a popular distribution channel for businesses looking to sell their products. With the rise of eCommerce and online shopping, some have predicted the decline of brick-and-mortar stores. However, retail stores remain a vital component of many companies' distribution strategies. Effective marketing is essential for companies looking to succeed in this channel. Here will discuss the importance of retail stores as a distribution channel and the role of marketing in driving sales. We will also explore trade marketing, its components, and how they help sell products in-store.

Retail Stores as a Distribution Channel

Retail stores are a vital link between businesses and consumers. They allow businesses to showcase their products and allow consumers to see, touch, and experience them before purchasing. In addition, they offer convenience for consumers, allowing them to purchase products on the spot without waiting for shipping or dealing with the hassle of returns.

Despite the growing popularity of eCommerce, retail stores remain an important distribution channel. According to a study by the National Retail Federation, in 2020, 83% of consumers made at least one in-store purchase, while only 60% made a purchase online. Retail stores offer a level of personalisation that online shopping cannot replicate. In-store sales associates can provide expert advice and recommendations, helping customers find the products that best fit their needs.

Moreover, retail stores have adapted to changing consumer preferences, offering a seamless shopping experience across channels. Many retailers now offer to buy online and pick up in-store options, allowing customers to order products online and pick them up at a nearby store. Others offer same-day delivery, providing the convenience of online shopping with the immediacy of in-store purchases.

Retail stores also serve as a valuable distribution channel for businesses looking to expand their reach. By partnering with retail stores, businesses can tap into the stores' existing customer bases and benefit from the stores' marketing and advertising efforts. Retailers often have established relationships with suppliers and distributors, making it easier for businesses to get their products into stores.

The Importance of Marketing in Retail Stores

Effective marketing is essential for businesses looking to succeed in retail stores. In-store marketing can help drive foot traffic, increase sales, and build brand awareness. With so many products competing for consumers' attention, businesses must find ways to stand out and differentiate themselves from their competitors.

One of the most effective ways to market products in retail stores is through point-of-sale (POS) displays. POS displays are promotional materials that are placed near the checkout or in other high-traffic areas of the store to grab the attention of shoppers. These displays can be used to showcase new or seasonal products, promote sales or discounts, or highlight specific features or benefits of a product. By placing these displays strategically, businesses can increase the chances of impulse purchases and boost sales.

Another important marketing tactic in retail stores is product packaging. Packaging plays a critical role in capturing consumers' attention and communicating a product's value proposition. Well-designed packaging can help differentiate a product from its competitors, create a strong brand identity, and communicate key features and benefits. For example, products with eye-catching colours, bold graphics, or unique shapes are likelier to stand out on shelves and catch consumers' attention.

In addition, businesses can leverage in-store promotions, such as coupons or loyalty programs, to drive sales and build customer loyalty. Offering discounts or rewards can incentivise customers to purchase, and a well-designed loyalty program can encourage repeat purchases and build long-term customer relationships.

Trade Marketing and its Components

Trade marketing is a subset of marketing focusing specifically on driving sales through retail channels. It aims to create strong relationships with retailers and optimise their in-store marketing efforts. There are several components of trade marketing that businesses need to consider when selling products in retail stores:

- **Retailer Relationships** with retailers are critical for successful trade marketing. Businesses need to understand the needs and preferences of each retailer and tailor their marketing efforts accordingly. For example, one retailer may prioritise low prices, while another may prioritise high-quality products or personalised service.

- **Merchandising** involves the layout and design of products in-store. Effective merchandising can help businesses capture consumers' attention, showcase their products effectively, and drive sales. This includes everything from product placement and packaging to signage and displays.

- **Promotions and pricing** are key components of trade marketing. Businesses must understand each retailer's pricing and promotion strategies and tailor their efforts accordingly. This may involve offering discounts or rebates, creating promotional displays, or leveraging loyalty programs to incentivise purchases.

- **Sales Enablement** involves providing retailers with the tools and resources to sell a product effectively. This may include product training, sales collateral, or promotional materials.

- **Analytics and Insights** are critical for optimising trade marketing efforts. By tracking sales data and analysing consumer behaviour, businesses can identify opportunities for improvement and refine their marketing strategies over time.

Effective marketing is essential for driving sales and building brand awareness in-store.

See also:

The Marketing Mix: Product
The Marketing Mix: Price
The Marketing Mix: Promotion
The Marketing Mix: Place
Consumer Behaviour: The Paradox of Choice
Consumer Behaviour: The Reciprocity Effect
Consumer Behaviour: Pareto's Principle

Chapter 45

Online Marketplace

Sales via online platforms have become increasingly popular in recent years, with the growth of eCommerce and the rise of digital technologies. For brands that focus on B2C or D2C business models, online platforms offer businesses a convenient and cost-effective way to reach a global audience and sell their products to customers worldwide. This chapter will explore the importance of marketing in online sales, as well as the role of analytics and customer data in driving growth.

The Importance of Marketing in Online Sales

Effective marketing is crucial for businesses looking to succeed in online sales. With so many products and services available online, businesses need to find ways to differentiate themselves from their competitors and capture consumers' attention.

One of the most important marketing tactics in online sales is search engine optimisation (SEO). SEO involves optimising a website's content and structure to rank higher in search engine results pages (SERPs). By ranking higher in SERPs, businesses can increase their visibility to potential customers and drive more website traffic.

In addition, businesses can leverage digital advertising to target specific audiences and drive traffic to their website. Social media advertising, pay-per-click (PPC) advertising, and display advertising are all effective ways to reach potential customers and drive sales.

Email marketing is another effective marketing tactic in online sales. Email campaigns can promote products, announce sales or discounts, and build customer loyalty. By building a strong email list and sending targeted, personalised messages, businesses can keep their brand top-of-mind with their customers and drive repeat purchases.

Key Elements To Consider

To succeed in online marketplaces, businesses need to consider several key elements that can help them optimise their listings and stand out from their competitors.

Product Images

Images are one of the most important elements of any online marketplace listing. High-quality images can help capture potential customers' attention and showcase the product's features and benefits. To optimise product images, businesses should:

- Use high-resolution images that show the product in detail from different angles.
- Use a white background to make the product stand out.
- Ensure that the images are optimised for fast loading times.
- Emphasise and increase the size of key information, such as multipack or product size, type, and brand.

Product Descriptions

Product descriptions are another critical component of online marketplace listings. A well-written product description can give customers important information about the product, including its features, benefits, and specifications. To optimise product descriptions, businesses should:

- Use clear and concise language that is easy to understand.
- Highlight the product's unique features and benefits.
- Use bullet points to break up the text and make it easier to read.
- Use keywords and phrases that customers are likely to search for.

Product Taxonomy

Product taxonomy refers to how products are categorised and organised within an online marketplace. Optimising product taxonomy can help businesses improve their listings' visibility and make it easier for customers to find their products. To optimise product taxonomy, businesses should:

- Use relevant and specific categories that accurately describe the product.
- Use subcategories to provide more detailed information about the product.
- Use product tags to help customers find products based on specific features or attributes.

Reviews and Ratings

Reviews and ratings are other decisive components of online marketplace listings. Positive reviews and high ratings can help build trust and credibility with potential customers, while negative reviews can have the opposite effect. To optimise reviews and ratings, businesses should:

- Encourage customers to leave reviews and ratings after purchasing the product.

- Respond promptly to any negative reviews to address customer concerns and improve the overall customer experience.
- Use customer feedback to make improvements to the product and address any issues that may be affecting sales.

Competitive Pricing

Pricing is a relevant factor in online marketplaces, where customers can access various products from different sellers. To optimise pricing, businesses should:

Research to determine the competitive landscape and identify the price range for similar products.

Use dynamic pricing strategies to adjust prices based on demand, seasonality, or other factors that may affect sales.

Offer discounts and promotions to incentivise customers to purchase the product.

When deciding which online marketplace to sell a particular product, businesses should consider various factors to ensure they choose the right platform for their needs.

Target Audience

The target audience is one of the most important factors when deciding which online marketplace to sell a product. Different marketplaces attract different types of customers, so businesses should choose a platform that aligns with their target audience. For example, suppose a business is targeting younger consumers. In that case, they may succeed on platforms like Instagram or TikTok, while businesses targeting older customers may succeed more on platforms like Amazon or eBay.

Product Type

The type of product being sold is another essential factor to consider when choosing an online marketplace. Some platforms are better suited for certain types of products than others. For example, handmade and unique items may do well on platforms like Etsy, while electronics and household items may perform better on Amazon or Walmart.

Marketplace Fees

Online marketplaces have different fee structures, impacting a business's bottom line. Before choosing a platform, businesses should carefully consider the fees associated with each platform and factor them into their pricing strategy.

Competition

Competition is another important factor when choosing an online marketplace. Some platforms may have more competition than others, making it more difficult for businesses to stand out and succeed. Businesses should research the competition on each platform they are considering and determine whether they can compete effectively.

Platform Features

Finally, businesses should consider the features and tools available on each online marketplace when deciding where to sell their products. Different platforms offer different features, such as advertising tools, analytics, and customer support, which can impact a business's ability to succeed.

Online marketplaces offer businesses a convenient and cost-effective way to reach a global audience and sell their products to customers worldwide.

See also:

The Marketing Mix: Pricing
The Marketing Mix: Place
Consumer Behaviour: The Paradox of Choice
Consumer Behaviour: Social Proof
Marketing Communication: Copy Writing
Marketing Communication: Search Engine Optimisation

eCommerce

eCommerce, short for electronic commerce, refers to buying and selling goods and services over the Internet. It has become a popular and convenient way for businesses to reach customers globally and for consumers to shop online from the comfort of their homes. This chapter provides an overview of the eCommerce basics, business models, and value delivery methods used for this channel.

While the topic of eCommerce is vast, we can boil it down to the following components:

- **Online Shopfront:** An online store or website where businesses display their products or services, and customers can browse, search, and make purchases.

- **Shopping Cart:** A virtual shopping cart that allows customers to add products or services to their cart, review their selections, and proceed to checkout.

- **Payment Gateway:** A secure online payment processing system that enables customers to make payments using various payment methods, such as credit/debit cards, e-wallets, or digital currencies.

- **Order Fulfilment:** The process of packing, shipping, and delivering products to customers after they purchase online.

- **Customer Service:** Providing support and assistance to customers before, during, and after their purchase, including handling inquiries, resolving issues, and managing returns/refunds.

- **Digital Marketing:** Strategies and tactics used to promote and drive traffic to the online store, such as search engine optimisation (SEO), social media marketing, email marketing, and pay-per-click (PPC) advertising.

eCommerce Business Models

Various eCommerce business models determine how products or services are sold online. Some standard eCommerce business models include:

B2C (Business-to-Consumer): The B2C eCommerce business model directly sells products or services to individual consumers. One of the advantages of this model is the potential for a large customer base, as it targets the general consumer market. It also allows for customisation and personalisation of the shopping experience. However, the competition can be fierce, and building brand awareness and customer trust can be challenging. Examples of B2C eCommerce businesses include Amazon, Walmart, and Nike.

B2B (Business-to-Business): The B2B eCommerce business model involves selling products or services to other businesses. One of the advantages of this model is the potential for more significant transactions and long-term contracts with business customers. It also allows for building long-term relationships with repeat business customers. However, B2B sales cycles can be longer and more complex, and the market may be more niche. Examples of B2B eCommerce businesses include Alibaba, Grainger, and Cisco.

C2C (Consumer-to-Consumer): The C2C eCommerce business model involves individuals selling products or services directly to other consumers. One of the advantages of this model is the ease of entry and low start up costs, as individuals can sell used or unwanted items. It also allows for a wide range of products and services available in the market. However, trust and safety concerns may arise, and building a reputable platform can be challenging. Examples of C2C eCommerce businesses include eBay, Etsy, and Facebook Marketplace.

Dropshipping: The dropshipping eCommerce business model involves selling products without owning or physically handling inventory. The retailer partners with a supplier who handles the fulfilment and shipping of products directly to the customer. One of the advantages of this model is low, upfront investment and inventory management. It also allows for a wide range of product options without warehousing. However, profit margins can be lowered, and reliance on suppliers for fulfilment can pose challenges regarding quality control and shipping times. Examples of dropshipping eCommerce businesses include Oberlo, Spocket, and Printful.

Subscription: The subscription eCommerce business model involves offering products or services repeatedly, typically with a monthly or annual subscription fee. One of the advantages of this model is predictable recurring revenue and customer retention. It also allows for customisation and personalisation of offerings based on customer preferences. However, acquiring and retaining customers can be challenging, and ensuring consistent product or service quality is crucial. Examples of subscription eCommerce businesses include Netflix, Dollar Shave Club, and Blue Apron.

Businesses should consider several factors when choosing their eCommerce business model. Some of the critical factors to consider include:

- **Target Market:** Understanding the target market and customer preferences is critical in selecting a suitable eCommerce business model. For example, a B2C model may be ideal for businesses targeting individual consumers, while a B2B model may be more appropriate for businesses selling to other companies.

- **Product or Service Offerings:** The type of product or service being offered can also influence the choice of the eCommerce business model. For instance, the dropshipping model may be ideal for businesses with a wide range of products, while a subscription model may be suitable for companies offering recurring services or products.

- **Pricing Strategy:** The pricing strategy can also impact the choice of an eCommerce business model. For example, a subscription model may be appropriate for businesses with a recurring revenue model, while a C2C model may be suitable for companies focusing on used or second-hand products.

- **Resource and Investment Requirements:** The resources and investment required for setting up and operating different eCommerce business models can vary significantly. For instance, the dropshipping model typically requires lower upfront investment than a B2B model, which may require higher inventory and infrastructure investments.

- **Competitive Landscape:** Analysing the competitive landscape is crucial in choosing a suitable eCommerce business model. Businesses should assess the competition, market demand, and consumer behaviour to determine which model aligns with their competitive advantage and business goals.

- **Operational Considerations:** The operational aspects of different eCommerce business models, such as fulfilment, inventory management, and customer service, should also be considered. For example, a dropshipping model may have lower operational complexities than a B2B model, which may involve long sales cycles and complex supply chains.

- **Growth and Scaling Potential:** The growth and scaling potential of the chosen eCommerce business model should also be considered. Businesses should assess the model's scalability in accommodating increased sales volume and xpanding into new markets.

Value Delivery Methods

Value delivery methods for eCommerce innovations refer to how businesses deliver value to their customers through innovative approaches in the eCommerce space. Here are some examples:

- **Free Shipping:** Offering free shipping to customers can be a value delivery method that encourages more purchases, reduces cart abandonment rates, and enhances the overall customer experience.

- **Same-day or Next-day Delivery:** Providing fast delivery options, such as same-day or next-day delivery, can be a value delivery method that appeals to customers who value convenience and speed.

- **Click-and-Collect:** Allowing customers to place an order online and pick it up at a nearby store or designated location can be a value delivery method that combines the convenience of online shopping with the immediacy of in-store pickup.

- **Customisation and Personalisation:** Offering customisable or personalised products or services can be a value delivery method that caters to individual customers' unique preferences and needs, enhancing their overall satisfaction and loyalty.

- **Subscription Models:** Implementing subscription-based business models can be a value delivery method that provides customers with recurring access to products or services, creating a predictable and convenient shopping experience.

- **Augmented Reality (AR) and Virtual Reality (VR):** Incorporating AR or VR technologies into the eCommerce experience can be a value delivery method that allows customers to try on products virtually, visualise how they would look in their environment, or experience virtual shopping environments.

- **Social Commerce:** Utilising social media platforms to sell products or services can be a value delivery method that leverages customers' social influence and engagement to drive sales and create a community of loyal customers.

These are just a few examples of value delivery methods for eCommerce innovations. Successful eCommerce businesses often leverage these and other innovative approaches to deliver value to their customers, enhance the overall shopping experience, and gain a competitive edge in the ever-evolving eCommerce landscape.

It's important to remember that building a successful eCommerce business takes time, effort, and continuous improvement. It's vital to keep learning, adapting, and refining strategies to achieve long-term success in the competitive eCommerce landscape.

When setting up an eCommerce business, companies should consider the business models and value delivery methods used for this channel.

See also:

The Marketing Mix: Pricing
The Marketing Mix: Place
Consumer Behaviour: The Paradox of Choice
Consumer Behaviour: Social Proof
Marketing Communication: Copy Writing
Marketing Communication: Search Engine Optimisation

VIII

Marketing Measurement

Chapter 47

Decide > Commit > Measure > Repeat

Marketing is an essential aspect of any business, and measuring the effectiveness of marketing campaigns is vital to ensure that resources are being used effectively. Measuring marketing involves assessing the performance of various marketing initiatives and evaluating their impact on the business's overall objectives. The importance of measurement in marketing cannot be overstated, and this section will explore some of the reasons why.

Benefits of Marketing Measurement

Helps In Making Informed Decisions

Measuring marketing performance provides valuable insights that can be used to make informed decisions. By analysing the results of different marketing campaigns, businesses can determine which strategies are effective and which are not. This information can be used to optimise marketing efforts and adjust plans to achieve better results.

Enables Accountability

Measuring marketing performance helps to create accountability within the marketing team. When marketing efforts are tracked and analysed, it becomes easier to identify the successes and failures of different campaigns. This information can be used to hold team members accountable for their actions and help ensure that everyone is working towards the same goals.

Provides A Benchmark for Future Campaigns

Measuring marketing performance provides a benchmark for future campaigns. By analysing the results of previous campaigns, businesses can set realistic goals and expectations for future initiatives. This information can be used to determine the level of investment required to achieve specific objectives and to track progress towards these goals.

Identifies Opportunities for Improvement

Measuring marketing performance helps to identify opportunities for improvement. By analysing the results of different campaigns, businesses can identify areas where performance could be improved. This information can be used to adjust strategies and optimise campaigns to achieve better results.

Provides Insight into Customer Behaviour

Measuring marketing performance provides valuable insights into customer behaviour. By analysing customer data, businesses can determine which campaigns resonate with their target audience and which are not. This information can be used to adjust strategies and create more targeted marketing initiatives that better address the needs and interests of customers.

Helps to Justify Marketing Spend

Measuring marketing performance helps to justify marketing spend. By tracking the results of different campaigns, businesses can determine the return on investment (ROI). This information can be used to demonstrate the value of marketing efforts and justify the level of investment required to achieve specific objectives.

Enables Data-Driven Decision-Making

Measuring marketing performance enables data-driven decision-making. By analysing the results of different campaigns, businesses can make decisions based on facts and figures rather than gut feelings or intuition. This approach can help minimise the risk of making inaccurate assumptions and lead to better outcomes.

Provides Insights Into the Competitive Landscape

Measuring marketing performance provides insights into the competitive landscape. Businesses can better understand how their competitors perform by analysing the results of different campaigns. This information can be used to adjust strategies and create more targeted marketing initiatives that better differentiate the business from its competitors.

Helps to Identify Trends

Measuring marketing performance helps to identify trends. Businesses can identify patterns and trends that inform marketing strategies by analysing data over time. This information can be used to adjust strategies and create more effective campaigns that better address changing customer needs and preferences.

Enables Continuous Improvement

Measuring marketing performance enables continuous improvement. By analysing the results of different campaigns, businesses can identify areas where performance could be improved and adjust strategies accordingly. This approach can help to optimise marketing efforts over time and achieve better results.

Key Steps to Marketing Measurement

However, measuring marketing performance can be challenging, and businesses need the right tools and processes to do it effectively.

Set Clear Objectives

Before measuring marketing performance, it's essential to set clear objectives that align with the business's overall goals. These objectives should be specific, measurable, achievable, relevant, and time-bound (SMART). By setting clear objectives, companies can track progress towards their goals and determine the effectiveness of their marketing initiatives.

Use the Right Metrics

To measure marketing performance effectively businesses need to use the right metrics to measure marketing performance effectively. Metrics should be relevant to the business's objectives and provide insights into the effectiveness of different marketing initiatives. Some standard marketing metrics include website traffic, conversion rates, click-through rates, engagement rates, and customer acquisition costs (CAC).

Track and Analyse Data

To measure marketing performance, businesses need to track and analyse data from different sources. This includes website analytics, social media analytics, email marketing analytics, and customer data. Companies can gain valuable insights into customer behaviour, campaign effectiveness, and the competitive landscape by analysing this data.

Use Marketing Automation Tools

Marketing automation tools can help businesses to track and analyse marketing performance more efficiently. These tools can automate lead generation, email marketing, social media management, and analytics tracking. By using these tools, businesses can save time and resources and gain more accurate insights into marketing performance.

Test and Optimise

Measuring marketing performance is not a one-time event, and businesses must continuously test and optimise their marketing initiatives to achieve better results. This involves A/B testing different campaigns, adjusting strategies based on data analysis, and constantly iterating on marketing efforts to improve performance over time.

Common Pitfalls

Focusing on Vanity Metrics

One of the most common mistakes businesses make when measuring marketing performance is focusing on vanity metrics. Vanity metrics may look impressive on the surface but do not provide meaningful insights into the effectiveness of marketing initiatives. For example, having many social media followers may look impressive, but it does not necessarily mean that these followers engage with the business or convert into customers. Businesses need to focus on metrics that align with their objectives and provide meaningful insights into the effectiveness of their marketing initiatives.

Not Setting Clear Objectives

Another common mistake businesses make is not setting clear objectives before measuring marketing performance. Without clear objectives, businesses may not know what metrics to track or how to interpret the data they collect. Setting clear objectives ensures that companies are tracking the right metrics and can determine the effectiveness of their marketing initiatives.

Overlooking the Customer Experience

Measuring marketing performance should not be limited to lead generation or sales metrics. It's also essential to track metrics related to the customer experience, such as customer satisfaction or retention. Overlooking the customer experience can lead to missed opportunities to improve customer loyalty and retention.

Not Considering the Big Picture

Measuring marketing performance should not be done in isolation. It's essential to consider the big picture, including the competitive landscape, industry trends, and other external factors that may impact marketing performance. Failing to consider the big picture can lead to misinterpretation of marketing data and missed opportunities to adjust marketing strategies.

Ignoring Data Quality

Finally, businesses may make the mistake of ignoring data quality when measuring marketing performance. Data quality refers to the accuracy, completeness, and consistency of data. If businesses collect data from multiple sources, they need to ensure that the data is accurate and consistent across sources. Failing to ensure data quality can lead to inaccurate insights and misguided marketing strategies.

The Importance of Quality Data

Identifying quality data in marketing is necessary for making informed decisions and optimising marketing performance. Quality data refers to accurate, complete, and consistent data, providing meaningful insights into marketing initiatives' effectiveness. Here are some tips for identifying quality data in marketing:

Use Reliable Sources

The first step in identifying quality data in marketing is to use reliable sources. This includes data from reputable sources such as Google Analytics, social media analytics tools, or email marketing platforms. It's also important to ensure that the data is current and up-to-date.

Check for Accuracy

Accuracy is essential for quality data. To ensure accuracy, it's important to check data against multiple sources and cross-reference it with other data points. For example, if marketers are tracking website traffic, they should check the website analytics against server logs to ensure the data is consistent.

Look for Completeness

Complete data provides a more comprehensive picture of marketing performance. It's important to ensure that data is complete, including all relevant data points and periods. Incomplete data can lead to inaccurate insights and misguided marketing strategies.

Ensure Consistency

Consistency is paramount regarding quality data. It's essential to ensure data consistency across all sources and periods.

Inconsistencies in data can lead to inaccurate insights and misguided marketing strategies.

Use Data Visualization

Data visualisation tools can help identify quality data by making it easier to spot patterns and trends. By visualising data, businesses can quickly identify outliers and inconsistencies and make informed decisions based on the insights gained from the data.

Use Machine Learning

Machine learning algorithms can help identify quality data by identifying patterns and trends that may not be apparent to humans. Machine learning can also identify outliers and anomalies in data, which can help businesses identify areas for improvement and optimise marketing strategies.

Measuring marketing performance the first step for businesses looking to optimise their marketing efforts and achieve their objectives.

See also:

Marketing Measurement: Key Performance Indicators
Marketing Measurement: The Balanced Scorecard

Chapter 48

Data Analysis

Throughout the book, we have highlighted the importance of data analysis several times. It's a common misconception that marketers don't have to work with numbers. Our field relies on strong analytical skills to ensure we direct and manage company resources as efficiently as possible. In this chapter, we will recap the key use cases of data analysis in marketing, look at a step-by-step guide on approaching it, and explore some essential Excel functions that come in handy when working with large data sets.

Data Analysis Use Cases

- **Customer Insights:** Data analysis helps marketers understand their customers, their preferences, and their behaviours. By analysing data, marketers can uncover patterns, trends, and correlations that provide valuable insights into customer demographics, buying habits, interests and needs. These insights enable marketers to create targeted and personalised marketing campaigns that resonate with their audience, leading to higher conversion rates and customer satisfaction.

- **Effective Decision-Making:** Marketing data analysis allows marketers to make data-driven decisions rather than relying on intuition or guesswork. Marketers can identify what works and doesn't by analysing marketing campaigns, customer response, sales performance, and market trends. This information helps them optimise marketing strategies, allocate resources effectively, and make informed decisions about pricing, product positioning, distribution channels, and promotional activities.

- **Campaign Optimisation:** Data analysis enables marketers to accurately measure a marketing campaign's effectiveness. By tracking and analysing key performance indicators (KPIs) such as click-through rates, conversion rates, customer acquisition costs, and return on investment (ROI), marketers can assess a campaign's success and identify improvement areas. They can refine their strategies, messaging, and targeting to optimise future campaigns and achieve better results.

- **Market Segmentation and Targeting:** Data analysis helps marketers segment their target market and identify distinct customer groups based on various criteria such as demographics, behaviours, interests, and purchasing power. By understanding these segments, marketers can tailor their marketing efforts to specific customer groups, delivering relevant messages and offers. This targeted approach improves the efficiency of marketing campaigns, reduces wastage of resources, and enhances customer engagement.

- **Competitive Advantage:** Data analysis provides a competitive advantage in today's competitive business landscape. Marketers who can effectively analyse data and derive actionable insights gain a deeper understanding of their market, competitors, and customers. This knowledge allows them to identify untapped opportunities, spot emerging trends, and stay ahead of the competition. By leveraging data analysis, marketers can make informed decisions that drive growth and help their organisations outperform rivals.

A Step-by-Step Guide to Data Analysis

Step 1: Organise and Clean Data

The first step in analysing data for a marketing campaign is to organise and clean the data. This involves removing duplicate or irrelevant data and ensuring that the data is consistent and accurate. Using a tool such as Microsoft Excel or Google Sheets is essential to organise the data and remove errors.

Step 2: Identify Patterns and Trends

Once the data is organised and cleaned, businesses need to identify patterns and trends in the data. This can be done using various tools such as data visualisation tools, pivot tables, or statistical software. Looking for trends and differences between segments or groups over time is important.

Step 3: Segment Data

Segmenting data helps identify patterns and trends within different groups or segments. This can be done based on various criteria, such as geographic location, demographics, or behaviour. Segmenting data can provide insights into which groups most respond to different marketing messages and tactics.

Step 4: Measure ROI

Measuring return on investment (ROI) is integral to analysing data for a marketing campaign. ROI is calculated by dividing the revenue generated by the campaign by the cost of the campaign. This provides insights into the campaign's profitability and can inform future investment in marketing initiatives.

Step 5: Test Hypotheses

Testing hypotheses help gain insights into the effectiveness of different marketing tactics. Hypotheses can be tested using A/B or multivariate testing to compare the performance of other marketing messages or tactic variations. This can provide insights into what works and what doesn't work in a marketing campaign.

Step 6: Make Data-Driven Decisions

Finally, businesses need to make data-driven decisions based on the insights gained from the data analysis. This involves using the insights to inform future marketing strategies and tactics. It's essential to continuously test and optimise marketing strategies to improve performance over time.

Data Analysis in Excel

Data analysis can be a smooth process, and Excel is a powerful tool to automate much of it daily. Marketers who master Excel should be the standard. Here are some tips on how to make Excel a helpful helper.

- **Use built-in functions:** Excel has many built-in functions for data analysis, such as SUM, AVERAGE, COUNT, MAX, MIN, and more. Familiarising oneself with these functions and using them to perform everyday data analysis tasks, such as calculations, aggregations, and filtering, can be helpful.

- **Utilise Excel's data analysis tools:** Excel also offers various data analysis tools, such as PivotTables, Data Tables, and What-If Analysis, which can assist in quickly analysing and summarising data, performing scenario analysis, and conducting sensitivity analysis, among other tasks.

- **Apply conditional formatting:** Conditional formatting is a powerful feature in Excel that allows users to apply different formatting styles to cells based on specific conditions. This feature can highlight trends, identify outliers, or visualise data for better analysis.

- **Sort and filter data:** Excel allows sorting and filtering data based on different criteria. Users can leverage these features to organise and analyse data based on specific attributes, such as sorting data by values, dates, or alphabetical order and filtering data to display only relevant information.

- **Use charts and graphs:** Excel offers a wide range of charts and graphs, such as bar charts, line charts, pie charts, and more, which can be used to present data in a visually appealing and meaningful way, making it easier to understand patterns and trends.

- **Clean and transform data:** Data in Excel may require cleaning and transformation before analysis. Excel's data cleaning tools, such as Text to Columns, Find and Replace, and Remove Duplicates, can clean and prepare data for analysis. Formulas and functions include CONCATENATE, LEFT, RIGHT, and SUBSTITUTE.

- **Validate data:** Ensuring data accuracy by validating data in Excel is essential. Data validation tools, such as data validation rules, can be used to define specific criteria for data entry and prevent errors, helping maintain data integrity and improving the reliability of the analysis.

- **Use Excel add-ins:** Excel offers various add-ins to enhance data analysis capabilities. For example, Power Query allows importing, cleaning, and transforming data from different sources, while Power Pivot enables advanced data modelling and analysis tasks. Exploring and utilising these add-ins can expand data analysis capabilities in Excel.

- **Learn keyboard shortcuts:** Excel has many shortcuts that can save time and improve efficiency. Familiarising oneself with commonly used shortcuts such as copying, pasting, formatting, and navigating through data can speed up data analysis workflows.

- **Document the analysis:** As with any data analysis task, documenting the analysis in Excel is important for transparency and reproducibility. Keeping track of the analysis steps, assumptions, and results in a separate sheet or document, and adding comments to formulas or cells to provide context for future reference, can be beneficial.

It is vital for marketers to be well versed with data analysis.

See also:

Market Analysis: Marketing Research
Market Analysis: Bias in Research
Marketing Measurement: Decide > Commit > Measure > Repeat
Marketing Measurement: Key Performance Indicators

Chapter 49

Key Performance Indicators

Key Performance Indicators, commonly known as KPIs, are critical for marketers to track and measure the success of their campaigns and overall marketing strategies. KPIs are specific metrics used to measure performance against clear business objectives. They help marketers identify improvement areas, monitor progress towards goals, and make data-driven decisions. KPIs also help to align marketing goals with broader business objectives, enabling marketers to demonstrate the value of marketing efforts to company executives. In this section, we will explore the importance of KPIs in marketing, the most important KPIs to track, and provide examples of each.

KPIs to Keep an Eye On

There are many KPIs that marketers can track, but not all of them are created equal. Some KPIs are more important than others, depending on the campaign's or strategy's objectives. Below are some of the most important KPIs that marketers should track.

Conversion Rate

This is the percentage of website visitors who take a specific action, such as purchasing or filling out a form. This metric is a critical KPI for marketers because it measures how effectively a website converts visitors into customers or leads. Optimising conversion rates allows marketers to drive more revenue and increase the effectiveness of their campaigns.

Example: If a website receives 1,000 monthly visitors and generates 50 leads, the conversion rate is 5%.

Cost Per Acquisition (CPA)

Cost Per Acquisition measures the cost of acquiring a new customer. This KPI is essential because it helps marketers evaluate their campaigns' profitability. By tracking CPA, marketers can determine which campaigns deliver the best return on investment and make data-driven decisions to optimise future campaigns.

Example: If a campaign costs $10,000 and generates 100 new customers, the CPA is $100.

Return on Investment (ROI)

Return on investment is the ratio of the net profit generated by a campaign to the total cost of the campaign. ROI is a crucial KPI because it helps marketers evaluate their campaigns' profitability and compare the effectiveness of different campaigns. By tracking ROI, marketers can determine which campaigns deliver the best return on investment and optimise future campaigns accordingly.

Example: If a campaign generates $20,000 in revenue and costs $10,000, the ROI is 100%.

Click-Through Rate (CTR)

Click-Through Rate measures the percentage of people who click on a link in an email, advertisement, or other marketing message. CTR is essential because it measures the effectiveness of marketing messages and campaigns. By tracking CTR, marketers can optimise their messaging and improve campaign performance.

Example: If an email campaign is sent to 10,000 people and generates 500 clicks, the CTR is 5%.

Customer Lifetime Value (CLV)

Customer Lifetime Value is the total revenue a customer will cause for a company over their lifetime. CLV is an essential KPI because it measures customers' long-term profitability and helps marketers make data-driven decisions on how much to invest in customer acquisition and retention efforts.

Example: If a customer spends $100 monthly on a subscription service and remains a customer for three years, the CLV is $3,600.

Social Media Engagement

Social Media Engagement measures users' interaction with social media content, such as likes, shares, and comments.

Social media engagement is essential because it measures the effectiveness of social media content and campaigns. Marketers can optimise their social media strategy and improve performance by tracking engagement.

Example: If a Facebook post receives 500 likes, 100 shares, and 50 comments, the engagement rate is 6%.

Referral

Referral is a marketing key performance indicator (KPI) that measures the number of customers or leads acquired through referrals from existing customers or external sources. Referral tracking is crucial as it helps businesses gauge the success of their referral programs and assess the effectiveness of word-of-mouth marketing strategies. By monitoring referral metrics, marketers can identify the sources generating the most referrals and allocate resources accordingly to nurture and incentivize these channels. Example: If a company receives 200 customer referrals from its existing client base and 50 referrals from external sources, the referral rate can be calculated as 250 referrals in total.

Bounce Rate

This measures the percentage of website visitors who leave a website after visiting only one page. This metric is an essential KPI because it measures the effectiveness of website design and content. By optimising the bounce rate, marketers can increase visitors' engagement and improve their campaigns' effectiveness.

Example: If a website receives 1,000 visitors and 500 leave after visiting only one page, the bounce rate is 50%.

Email Open Rate

The Email Open Rate measures the percentage of recipients who open an email. Email Open Rate is essential because it measures the effectiveness of email subject lines and overall email strategy. By tracking the open email rate, marketers can optimise their email strategy and improve the performance of their campaigns.

Example: If an email campaign is sent to 10,000 people and 2,000 people open the email, the open email rate is 20%.

Net Promoter Score (NPS)

Net Promoter Score is a customer satisfaction metric that measures the likelihood of customers recommending a company to their friends and family. NPS is essential because it measures customer loyalty and satisfaction with a company's products or services. By tracking NPS, marketers can identify areas for improvement and make data-driven decisions to improve customer satisfaction.

Example: If a company has an NPS score of 50%, 50% of customers will likely recommend the company to their friends and family.

To avoid data fatigue, it is recommended to understand which KPIs need to be reviewed on a daily, weekly or monthly basis, which will help drive focus and help avoid misinterpretation of data.

Limitations of KPIs

While KPIs are essential for measuring marketing efforts' success, they have limitations. They provide a snapshot of performance at a particular moment but are not always comprehensive and can be influenced by external factors beyond a marketer's control. It's important to remember that the KPIs highlighted here should be used with other data sources and qualitative feedback to view campaign performance comprehensively.

If it's not measured, it can't be improved.

See also:

Marketing Measurement: Decide > Commit > Measure > Repeat
Marketing Measurement: Data Analysis
Glossary

Chapter 50

The Balanced Scorecard Framework

The Balanced Scorecard (BSC) is a management tool that helps businesses to measure and manage performance across four key perspectives: financial, customer, internal processes, and learning and growth. Developed by Robert S. Kaplan and David P. Norton in the 1990s, the BSC has become a widely used framework for businesses to align their strategies with their goals and objectives.

Here is an overview of each of the four perspectives in the Balanced Scorecard, along with examples of metrics and targets that businesses might use to measure their performance:

Financial Perspective: This perspective focuses on financial metrics such as revenue, profit, and return on investment (ROI). Metrics might include:

- Revenue growth rate: The percentage increase in revenue over a specified period.
- Profit margin: The percentage of revenue that is profit.
- Return on investment (ROI): The net profit ratio to the investment amount.

Example target: Increase revenue by 10% and maintain a profit margin of at least 15% over the next fiscal year.

Customer Perspective: This perspective focuses on customer satisfaction, loyalty, and retention metrics. Metrics might include:

Net Promoter Score (NPS): A metric that measures customer loyalty and willingness to recommend the brand to others.

Customer retention rate: The percentage of customers who continue to use the product or service.

Customer satisfaction score (CSAT): A metric that measures customers' satisfaction with the product or service.

Example target: Achieve an NPS score of 75 and a customer retention rate of 80% over the next fiscal year.

Internal Processes Perspective: This perspective focuses on metrics related to the efficiency and effectiveness of internal business processes. Metrics might include:

- Cycle time: The time it takes to complete a process, such as order processing or production.
- Error rate: The percentage of errors or defects in a process.
- Employee productivity: The amount of output per employee.

Example target: Reduce cycle time by 20% and maintain an error rate of less than 2% over the next fiscal year.

Learning and Growth Perspective: This perspective focuses on employee training, development, and innovation metrics. Metrics might include:

- Employee engagement: The level of commitment and motivation among employees.
- Training hours per employee: The time spent on training and development per employee.
- Innovation rate: The percentage of revenue generated by new products or services.

Example target: Increase employee engagement by 10% and spend at least 20 hours per employee on training and development over the next fiscal year.

The Balanced Scorecard framework provides a comprehensive and balanced approach to measuring business performance across multiple perspectives. By setting targets and tracking metrics in these four areas, businesses can ensure that they are aligned with their strategic goals and objectives and can make informed decisions to drive growth and improve performance.

Benefits of the BSC

The Balanced Scorecard (BSC) framework has several benefits and limitations, which are essential to consider when implementing this approach to measure and manage business performance.

- **Comprehensive approach:** The BSC framework provides a comprehensive and balanced approach to measuring business performance across multiple perspectives, including financial, customer, internal processes, and learning and growth. This enables businesses to identify opportunities for improvement across all areas of the organisation and to align their strategies with their goals and objectives.

- **Better decision-making:** Businesses can make informed decisions based on data and evidence by tracking and analysing critical metrics across multiple perspectives. This can lead to more effective allocation of resources, better prioritisation of initiatives, and improved performance overall.

- **Aligning objectives:** The BSC framework enables businesses to align their objectives and strategies with their mission and vision, ensuring that all stakeholders work towards a common goal. This can help to improve communication, collaboration, and accountability across the organisation.

- **Focus on continuous improvement:** The BSC framework emphasises the importance of continuous improvement, encouraging businesses to monitor and adjust their performance over time. This helps to ensure that businesses remain competitive and responsive to changing market conditions.

Limitations of the Balanced Scorecard Framework

- **Complex implementation:** Implementing the BSC framework can be complex and time-consuming, requiring significant resources and investment. This may be challenging for smaller businesses or those with limited resources.

- **Data availability:** The BSC framework relies heavily on data and metrics to measure and track performance across multiple perspectives. If businesses cannot access reliable and accurate data, it may be challenging to implement this framework effectively.

- **Limited focus on external factors:** The BSC framework focuses primarily on internal factors such as financial performance, customer satisfaction, and internal processes. While these are important metrics, they may not capture the impact of external factors such as market trends, regulatory changes, or competitive pressures.

- **Over-emphasis on short-term goals:** The BSC framework can sometimes lead businesses to focus too heavily on short-term goals and metrics at the expense of longer-term strategic objectives. This can lead to a lack of focus on essential issues such as innovation, sustainability, or employee development.

The BSC framework can be a powerful tool for businesses to align their strategies with their goals and objectives.

See also:

Market Analysis: Marketing Research
Market Analysis: Bias in Research
Marketing Measurement: Data Analysis

Glossary

6Ps: Product, Price, Place, Promotion, People, and Process - A marketing framework that encompasses the key elements in developing and implementing a marketing strategy.

AR: Augmented Reality - A technology that superimposes computer-generated elements, such as images, videos, or sound, onto the real-world environment, enhancing the user's perception and interaction with the surroundings.

A/B Testing: Process used to compare two versions of a marketing campaign to determine which one performs better. Often used to optimise website design or email campaigns.

API: Application Programming Interface - A set of rules that allows two computer programs to communicate with each other. Used to integrate different systems, track data and automate processes.

AOV: Average Order Value - This is the average amount of money customers spend per purchase. Often used to understand customer purchase behaviour.

B2B: Business-to-Business - A transaction or relationship between two businesses, such as a manufacturer selling products to a retailer.

B2C: Business-to-Consumer - A transaction or relationship between a business and individual consumers, such as a retailer selling products directly to customers.

Basket Size: Refers to the average value or number of items purchased by a customer in a single transaction. It measures the amount of goods or services a customer buys during a specific visit to a store or an online shopping session.

BOFU: Bottom of Funnel - This is the last stage of the consumer journey with a brand. At this stage, customers are ready to make a purchase decision. See TOFU and MOFU.

BSC: Balanced Scorecard - A strategic performance measurement framework that considers various aspects of an organization's performance, including financial, customer, internal processes, and learning and growth perspectives.

BR: Brand Recognition - The awareness and familiarity consumers have with a particular brand.

CMS: Content Management System - A software platform that allows users to create, manage, and publish digital content on websites.

CMO: Chief Marketing Officer - The senior executive responsible for developing and implementing an organisation's marketing strategies and overseeing marketing activities.

CMS: Content Management System - A software application that allows users to create, store and manage digital content. Often used to develop and maintain websites, or social media content.

Conversion Rate: Percentage of website visitors that complete the desired action, such as subscribing to an email list or making a purchase.

CPA: Cost-per-Acquisition - A marketing metric calculating the average cost of acquiring a new customer or lead.

CPC: Cost-per-Click - A marketing metric determining the average cost an advertiser pays for each click on an online advertisement.

CPL: Cost-per-Lead - A marketing metric that measures the average cost incurred to generate a new lead.

CPM: Cost-per-Mille - A marketing metric determining the average cost incurred for one thousand impressions of an advertisement. Typical pricing structure in online advertising.

CRM: Customer Relationship Management - Software/system used for managing relationships with potential or existing customers.

CSAT: Customer Satisfaction - A metric that measures the level of satisfaction or contentment of customers with a product, service, or overall experience.

CTA: Call-to-Action - A statement or instruction that encourages users or viewers to take a specific action, such as clicking a link, making a purchase, or subscribing to a newsletter.

CTR: Click-through Rate - Measures the number of people who click on an ad or a link divided by the total number of people who view it.

CRO: Conversion Rate Optimisation - Process of improving the conversion rate of website visitors. This involved analysing user behaviour, testing various website designs and optimising landing pages.

DAB: Digital Audio Broadcasting - Digital radio transmission technology enables the broadcast of high-quality audio content, offering a wider selection of stations and improved reception compared to traditional analogue radio.

D2C: Direct-to-Consumer - A business model where companies sell their products or services directly to consumers without intermediaries or retailers.

EEAT: Experience, Expertise, Authoritativeness, Trustworthiness - Framework by Google used to evaluate the quality and credibility of content, particularly in the context of YMYL (Your Money or Your Life) topics.

Frequency: Refers to the number of times an individual or target audience is buying a product or is exposed to a specific advertisement or marketing message within a given time period, such as a week or month.

Gated Content: Content that requires a user to submit contact information before they can access it. Often used to capture leads and build email lists.

GRPs: Gross Rating Points - Metric used in advertising to quantify the total reach and frequency of an advertising campaign by multiplying the reach percentage by the average frequency of exposure.

ICP: Ideal Customer Profile - This is a detailed description of the type of customer an organisation should be targeting.

ILV: Inbound Lead Velocity - The rate at which new leads are generated. Used to measure the success of a campaign.

KPI: Key Performance Indicator - A quantifiable metric used to measure the performance and effectiveness of specific activities or objectives within a business.

KISS: Keep It Simple, Stupid - A principle that advocates for simplicity and avoiding unnecessary complexity in design, communication, or problem-solving.

Lead Gen: Lead Generation - Process of acquiring new leads for the business. This can be done through content marketing, PPC campaigns or other marketing strategies.

Lead Magnet: Incentive to attract leads and build email lists. This can be anything from digital downloads to free courses or trials.

LTV: Lifetime Value - A metric that predicts the total revenue a customer will generate over their entire relationship with a business.

NPS: Net Promoter Score - A metric used to assess customer loyalty and gauge the likelihood of customers recommending a company or its products/services to others. It is based on a survey asking customers to rate their likelihood of recommending on a scale of 0 to 10.

MAT: Moving Annual Total - A measure that calculates the total of a metric over a rolling 12-month period.

MECE: Mutually Exclusive, Collectively Exhaustive - A framework or approach used to organize and analyze marketing strategies or market segments. It ensures that the categories or segments created are distinct from each other (mutually exclusive) and collectively cover the entire target market (collectively exhaustive).

MOFU: Middle of Funnel - The second stage of the consumer journey with a brand. At this stage, consumers are starting to evaluate the brand and consider their options. See TOFU and BOFU.

MoM: Month-over-Month - A comparison of data or performance metrics between two consecutive months to identify changes, trends, or growth.

MQL: Marketing Qualified Lead - Leads that have undergone initial qualification and are ready to be passed on to the sales teams. These leads typically have some sort of engagement with the company.

MVP: Minimum Viable Product - The most basic version of a product developed and released with minimum features to gather feedback and validate its viability in the market.

OOH: Out-of-Home - Refers to advertising and promotional activities that target audiences outside their homes, such as billboards, transit ads, street furniture ads, and digital signage.

Organic Traffic: Traffic (volume of visitors) that comes from unpaid search results or other channels. Often generated through SEO or other content marketing activities. The opposite would be 'paid traffic'.

Penetration: Refers to the process of entering and gaining a larger share of an existing market with existing products or services. It involves increasing market share by attracting customers away from competitors or enticing non-users to become customers.

PESTLE: Political, Economic, Social, Technological, Legal, and Environmental - A framework for analysing and monitoring external factors and trends that can impact an organisation's business environment and strategy.

PFP: Pay-for-Performance - An advertising model where advertisers only pay for results such as downloads or form submissions.

PPC: Pay-per-Click - An online advertising model in which advertisers pay a fee each time their ad is clicked. It is commonly used in search engines, display, and social media advertising.

PR: Public Relations - Managing and maintaining an organisation's positive public image and reputation through various communication channels and strategies.

PPV: Pay-per-View - An online advertising model where advertisers pay for the views of their ads instead clicks.

QR Code: Quick Response Code - This is a type of barcode that a smartphone can scan. Often used to redirect customers to a website or digital content.

Reach: Measures the total number or percentage of unique individuals or households exposed to a specific marketing campaign, advertisement, or media channel within a given period.

Retargeting: A form of advertising that targets users based on their previous online behaviour. Often used to encourage users who have abandoned a shopping cart to complete their purchase.

ROI: Return on Investment - A financial metric that measures the profitability or return generated from an investment.

ROAS: Return on Advertising Spend - A metric that measures the effectiveness of advertising campaigns by comparing the revenue generated to the cost of the advertising.

RT: Retweet/Repost - When a user reposts another user's tweet. A key mechanic on social media channels that can help increase visibility and engagement.

RTB: Reason to believe - A marketing term referring to the evidence or persuasive elements supporting a product or brand's claims, fostering consumer credibility and trust.

SERP: Search Engine Results Page - The page a search engine displays in response to a user's search query shows a list of relevant web pages.

SEO: Search Engine Optimization - Optimising a website or online content to improve its visibility and ranking in search engine results pages.

SEM: Search Engine Marketing - A form of online marketing that involves promoting a website or web pages by increasing their visibility in search engine result pages through paid advertising, such as pay-per-click campaigns.

SMB: Small and Medium-sized Business - A business classification that includes companies with a moderate level of revenue, employees, and operational scale.

SME: Small and Medium-sized Enterprise - A business classification that includes companies with a relatively small number of employees and less revenue than larger corporations.

SMM: Social Media Marketing - Is the process of using social media platforms to promote a product or service.

SQL: Sales Qualified Lead - Leads that have met all the criteria to be considered qualified for sale. Typically further along in the sales cycle and have a greater chance of becoming customers.

SWOT: Strengths, Weaknesses, Opportunities, and Threats - A strategic analysis framework used to assess and evaluate the internal and external factors that can impact the performance and competitiveness of an organisation.

TOFU: Top of Funnel - The first stage of the customer journey with a brand. Customers are learning about the brand and considering their options.

UGC: User Generate Content - Content created by users and shared on social media or a company's website. Can increase brand awareness, build trust and improve customer engagement.

UI: User Interface - The visual and interactive elements of a software application or website that users interact with to perform tasks and access information.

Upsell: A sales technique that encourages customers to purchase more expensive or higher-value items. Can increase customer lifetime value and revenue.

URL: Uniform Resource Locator - A web address that identifies a specific page or file on the internet. Often used in marketing to track clicks, engagement, and optimise campaigns.

USP: Unique Selling Proposition - A unique feature, benefit, or characteristic of a product or service that sets it apart from competitors and provides a compelling reason for customers to choose it.

UVP: Unique Value Proposition - A statement that defines the unique benefits and values a product or service offers customers, differentiating it from competitors.

UX: User Experience - A measure of how users interact with a website or product. Encompasses all aspects of a user experience.

Vanity Metric: A metric that measures activity but not success. Examples include website visits, downloads, or social media followers.

VR: Virtual Reality - A technology that creates a simulated, computer-generated environment that can be experienced and interacted with by a user through special equipment, such as a headset or goggles.

WOM: Word of Mouth - The act of individuals recommending or discussing a product, service, or brand with others, typically based on their own positive experiences or opinions.

YTD: Year-to-Date - A period that starts from the beginning of the current year and extends up to the present date. It tracks and compares performance or financial data within a specific year.

YoY: Year-over-Year - A comparison of data or performance metrics between the same period in two consecutive years. It is used to measure growth or changes over time.

Index

F

Facebook, 86, 98, 153, 219, 221, 265, 291, 296
feedback, 49, 98, 103, 132, 164, 264–65, 273, 356
feedback forms, 265
fees, 291, 311, 356
fee structures, 311
filter data, 335
focus groups, 26, 85, 90, 95–97, 103–5, 131, 149
followers, 184–85, 266, 269, 271–73, 327, 363
forces, 5, 59, 61, 64
  competitive, 59, 64
  dominant, 249
  technological, 64
Ford, 105
framework, 25, 31, 57, 59–60, 62, 125–28, 133, 157, 159, 176, 345, 347–48, 355–56

G

Geico, 118
gender, 83, 85–87, 92, 168, 246
Geographic Segmentation, 83
gifts, 193, 195–96
globalisation, 64
Glossier, 114, 267
goals, 94, 97, 142, 147, 219, 221, 259–60, 324, 326, 339, 345, 347, 349
Good copywriting, 211–12, 214–15
Good Marketing Insights, 93–94

good publicity, 209
goods, 55, 139, 233, 352
Google, 265, 283, 287–89, 291, 354
Google Ads, 221, 291
Google Ads Keyword Planner, 294
Google Alerts, 265
Google Analytics, 289, 329
Google's EEAT methodology, 283
grab, 147, 229, 252, 302
graphics, 212, 278, 294
group of customers, 71, 76, 82, 119, 332
group of people, 86–87, 96
groups, 35, 82–83, 96, 183, 333
growth, 26, 59, 96, 102, 167, 258, 307, 317, 345, 347, 355
Guerilla advertising, 245
guerrilla marketing, 220
guest blogging, 286, 289
guidance, 52, 57, 64

H

habits, 84–85, 331
health, 51, 237, 260–61
heuristics, 179, 188
higher rankings, 284–85, 287
history of marketing, 5, 17
history of print advertising, 233
History of Radio Advertising, 249

I

clear, 294, 326, 328
initial, 259
measurable, 294
offensive stereotypes,
    avoiding, 35
online, 39, 78, 96, 204–6,
    265–66, 291, 302, 307,
    313–14, 353, 356–57
online behaviour, 293–94,
    357
Online Marketplace Product
    Distribution, 156, 191,
    289
online marketplaces, 7, 152,
    155, 186, 307–12
online platforms, 13, 227, 307
online shopping, 155, 301–2,
    318
opportunities, 43, 47–52, 56,
    102, 149, 167, 226, 237,
    250–51, 324, 332
optimising, 38, 283–86, 307,
    342, 353, 358
organisation, 9, 29, 41–42,
    63, 82, 157, 257–62,
    347–48, 354, 356, 358
organisational culture, 36
outcomes, 9, 39, 41, 103, 111,
    197
Ozzy Osbourne, 82

P
packaging, 36, 129–30, 133–
    35, 161, 175, 206, 303–4
packaging design, 135
packaging features, 135
pages, 10, 91, 153, 164, 289,
    342, 357, 359

about us, 283
landing, 295–97, 353
website's, 287
paradox of choice, 6, 187–90,
    305
Pareto's Principle, 6, 197, 305
partnering, 125, 155, 185,
    222, 270, 302
partnerships, 155, 185, 272
Patagonia, 118
patterns, 90, 97, 100, 197,
    325, 331, 333, 335
pay-per-click. *See* PPC
Pay-Per-Click Advertising, 6,
    150, 291
perceived value, 27, 75–76,
    125, 140–41, 174–76
perceptions, 141–42, 162,
    168, 173, 179–80
performance, 42, 116, 132,
    323–25, 327, 334, 341–
    43, 345, 347–48, 354,
    358, 360
performance metrics, 355,
    360
personalisation, 19, 116, 189,
    194–95, 276, 301, 314,
    316, 318
personality, 82, 117, 130,
    133, 135, 168, 254, 272,
    274
PESTLE Framework, 5, 53
P&G, 9, 12, 134
Pharrell Williams, 255
phenomenon, 181–82, 187
phrases, 17, 211, 215, 285,
    292, 294, 309

innovative, 140, 159, 206
multiple, 141–42
new, 47, 53, 60, 86–87, 126,
    131, 141, 143, 260–61,
    271–72, 279–80
sustainable, 54, 56
product type, 25, 311
professional advertising
    services, 234
profitability, 55, 59, 84, 137,
    140, 144–45, 198, 340,
    357
profit margins, 315, 345
profits, 23, 59, 62, 70, 140,
    175, 194, 345
proliferation, 226, 250
promotional materials, 223,
    229, 302, 304
promotional strategy, 129,
    149–50
promotion and distribution,
    204
promotions, 125–26, 142,
    147–48, 150, 170, 174–
    75, 188, 203–6, 210, 270,
    276–77, 304–5, 310
proof, 120, 232
prototype, 131–32
publicity stunt, 196
public relations, 6, 23, 27,
    125, 147–48, 204, 206,
    257, 356

Q

quality, 61–63, 67, 69, 71,
    76–77, 83, 117, 120, 133,
    137, 157
queries, 218

questionnaire, 98

R

radio, 17, 109, 147, 203–5,
    235, 249–51, 253, 256
rates, 196, 340, 353–55
ratings, 184–85, 309
readership, 237–38
reciprocity effect, 6, 193–96
recognition, 226, 257, 297
recommendations, 19, 64,
    144, 189, 263, 266, 272,
    302
referrals, 264, 341–42
relevance, 225, 239–41, 252,
    286, 291–92
representation, 237
reputation, 110–11, 117, 159,
    195, 258, 284, 356
research, 5, 85, 87, 94–97,
    101, 103–5, 169, 179,
    204, 212, 310–11
retailers, 17, 60, 144–45,
    153–54, 170, 302–3
retail stores, 28, 152, 155,
    159, 301–3
return, 42, 193, 295, 340, 345,
    357
revenue, 55, 110–11, 197–98,
    270, 280, 283, 285, 333,
    339–40, 345–46, 357–59
reviews, 13–14, 17, 20, 42,
    54, 184, 215, 279, 284,
    309, 313
risks, 53–54, 56, 67, 102, 164,
    325

About the Author

Sonya is an award-winning marketer with nine years of experience in the industry. Having worked for internationally renowned companies such as Müller Dairy, Henkel, Ferrero, and TikTok, she has developed a deep understanding of marketing strategy and branding.

Beyond her corporate career, Sonya is also a passionate podcaster, university guest lecturer and online educator. As a TikTok Creator with more than 60,000 followers, Sonya has gained recognition for her ability to demystify marketing in a fun and approachable way and make it more accessible to all.

She loves to hear from readers. You can email her via gonzalezmier.sonya@gmail.com or leave a review on Amazon.

Printed in Great Britain
by Amazon

27068816R00215